W9-AGM-497

IN THE ERA OF
HUMAN CAPITAL

IN THE ERA OF HUMAN CAPITAL

The Emergence of Talent, Intelligence,
and Knowledge as the Worldwide
Economic Force and What It Means
to Managers and Investors

Richard Crawford

 HarperBusiness
A Division of HarperCollins*Publishers*

HC
79
T4
C73
1991

International Standard Book Number: 0–88730–506–7

Library of Congress Catalog Card Number: 91–9552

Printed in the United States of America

Library of Congress Cataloging-in-Publication Data

Crawford, Richard, 1946-
    In the era of human capital : the emergence of talent,
  intelligence, and knowledge as the worldwide economic force and what
  it means to managers and investors / Richard Crawford.
      p.   cm.
    Includes index.
    ISBN 0–88730–506–7
    1. Technological innovations—Economic aspects.   2. Information
  society.   3. Human capital.   4. Investment analysis.
  5. Investments.   I. Title.
  HC79.T4C73   1991
  338′.064—dc20   91–9552
                                                         CIP

91 92 93 94 CC/HC 9 8 7 6 5 4 3 2 1

Contents

Dedicated to Robin, a true champion,
from whom I learned
the world was changing

Acknowledgments

I could not have completed this book without the many people who typed portions of the manuscript and exhibits, read and commented on drafts of the manuscript, and assisted in the editing. In particular, I would like to thank Alec Horniman, Les Grayson, Bill Sihler, Casey Opitz, Carolyn Lyons, Kate Feeney, Mike Zirkle, and Marie Payne, of the Darden Graduate School of Business Administration at the University of Virginia; my personal friends Nick Miller, Ed Brownfield, Katrina Sherrerd, Peggy Clarity, and Tom Burnham; my father, Claude Crawford; and Mark Greenberg, Martha Jewett, and Jen Fleissner of my publisher, HarperBusiness. Both the physical assistance and the moral support they provided me with were critical to the completion of the book. Further, I would like to thank the Darden Graduate Business School whose library and other research facilities were invaluable to me in developing this book.

I

THE CHANGING ECONOMIC AND BUSINESS ENVIRONMENT

1

The Dawn of the Knowledge Economy

This book is about change. From the mid-1960s to the present we have experienced the most rapid period of technological, economic, and social change in history, and change in the next twenty-five years should be even more rapid and stressful. Major companies that took a century to build disappear in a year. Countries that nobody paid much attention to emerge as new powers in the world economy or major threats to its stability. Basic social structure is transformed as singles, single-parent families, and blended families replace traditional families. And technological advances in computers, communications, materials, and biotechnology proliferate at an ever increasing pace.

These changes have arisen from a massive transformation of the global economy. As Third World countries go through the process of industrialization, the advanced industrial economies of Western Europe, North America, and Japan are rapidly evolving into postindustrial knowledge economies. In the new knowledge economy information and knowledge replace physical and financial capital as the major competitive advantages in business. Creative intelligence underlies the wealth of the new society.

This may not be news to you. You are well educated and travel regularly. You routinely buy and read general newspapers and magazines like the *New York Times* and *Time* and business publications like the *Wall Street Journal* and *Fortune*. You read a wide range of business and nonbusiness books. And you routinely watch television news and TV programs about economic and business issues.

You are aware that the world has changed dramatically since World War II, and you are familiar with the concept that the United States has an information economy. Further, you have some understanding of advanced computer and communications technology. You either use a computer at work and home or supervise people using computers. Similarly, you use fax machines and a variety of advanced telecommunications features like voice mail and international direct dialing. You may be less familiar with other types of advanced technology, such as robotics, biotechnology, and advanced material and energy technology, but you have probably either read some business articles about these subjects or seen TV programs about them.

Despite all this, you may not fully understand what an information economy is or may wonder about its significance. Although you are aware of dramatic economic and social change (possibly painfully so in your personal life), you may not grasp what is causing the change or where it will lead. And while you are quite familiar with advanced technology, you may wonder what its long-term impact will be. This book answers some of these questions about what is happening and why.

More is known about the causes of this global transformation than you may realize. Economic historians studying the general development of the world economy, and particularly the development of the industrial world over the last 250 years, have developed a model of how economies and societies evolve. The model is as follows: new knowledge leads to new technology, which in turn leads to economic changes, which in turn lead to social and political changes, which ultimately create a new *paradigm,* or view of the world. This model can be used to explain the dramatic economic, social, and political changes the world is experiencing.

This book can help you create a new vision. The first part provides a broad overview of the new society that is being created by the technological, economic, and social changes that are being experienced in North America, Europe, and Japan, and the causes of those changes. In the second section I discuss the impact of these changes on business, with particular focus on U.S. business. And in the third section I discuss how these changes affect finance and investment, with attention to both broad macroeconomic policy issues and specific investment implications. It is impossible, however, to discuss all facets of global change adequately in a single book. I have intended to provide you with a framework that you can use to further your own understanding of past and future global change. I hope that I have accomplished my goal.

Table 1.1 uses this model to summarize the key technological, economic, social, political, and paradigm (or world view) characteristics of the four basic types of societies—primitive, agricultural, industrial, and, most recently, knowledge. This book focuses primarily on explaining the differences between industrial and knowledge societies. The arrows illustrate the evolution of society from primitive to agricultural to industrial to knowledge and the relationship between technological, economic, social, political, and paradigm change.

Human capital—that is, skilled, educated people—is central in the global transformation. Although the concept of human capital was known to Adam Smith and other economists as early as the eighteenth century, serious work on the economic theory of human capital is quite new. The term *human capital* first appeared in economic literature in 1961 in an article titled "Investment in Human Capital" by Nobel Prize–winning economist Theodore W. Schultz in the *American Economic Review*.

Several economists, the most prominent of whom were Schultz and Gary Becker, have since done extensive work on the economic theory of human capital. Becker's book *Human Capital* was published in 1964, and Schultz's book *Investment in Human Capital* was published in 1971. Although the economic theory of human capital has been further developed in recent years, little has been written about how the concepts of human capital apply to the daily problems of business. This book tries to fill that need by examining what this evolution means to you as an employee or executive.

The changes that are occurring are stressful for many people, but transforming the world to a knowledge economy is probably the most hopeful step taken in the history of the world's economic development. For most of the world's people this develop-

Table 1.1   Key Characteristics of Four Basic Societies

	Primitive Society →	Agricultural Society →	Industrial Society →	Knowledge Society
Technology	Energy: human energy Materials: animal skins, stones Tools: minimal for cutting/pounding (normally made of stone) Production methods: none Transportation system: walking Communication system: speech	Energy: natural (human, animal, wind) Materials: renewable resources (trees, cotton, wool) Tools: amplify human muscle (levers and winches) or harness natural forces (sail, waterwheel) Production methods: handcraft Transportation system: horse, wagon, sailing ship Communication system: handwriting	Energy: fossil fuels (oil, coal) Materials: nonrenewable resources (metals, etc.) Tools: machines to replace human muscles (engines) Production method: assembly line and interchangeable parts Transportation system: steamship, railroad, auto, and airplane Communication system: printing, TV	Energy: natural (sun, wind), nuclear Materials: renewable resources (biotechnology), ceramics, recycling Tools: machines to assist mind (computers and related electronics) Production methods: robotics Transportation system: spaceship Communication system: unlimited individual communications through electronic medium
Economy	Gathering, hunting, or fishing	Decentralized self-sufficient local economy whose central economic activity is production and consumption of food with no market activity of significance Simple division of labor organized around village with few, clearly defined levels of authority (nobility, priests, warriors, slaves, or serfs) Land the primary resource in economy	National mass market economy whose central economic activity is the production of standardized, tangible things with split between production and consumption Complex division of labor built on narrow specialized skills, standard work pattern, and synchronization organized in large hierarchical institutions with many levels of authority Physical capital the primary resource	Integrated global economy whose central economic activity is the provision of knowledge services with more fusion of producer and consumer Organized around small entrepreneurial network organizations in which members have a direct gain sharing interest Human capital the primary resource
Social system	Small bands or tribes	Immobile extended family with clear definition of sexual roles and the family the primary support system Education limited to elite	Nuclear family with split sexual roles and immortal institutions the primary support system Social values emphasize conformity, elitism, and class Mass education completed by adulthood	Individual central with multiple family types and fusing of sexual roles with self-help emphasis and mortal institutions Social values emphasize diversity, egalitarism, individualism Education individualized and continuous
Political system	Tribe the basic political unit in which tribal elders and chief rule	Feudalism: law, religion, social class, and politics geared to management of land with authority by birth (aristocracy rules), local community the basic political unit	Capitalism and Marxism: law, religion, social class, and politics shaped by concerns about ownership and control of capital investment Nationalism: strong central rational government in the form of either representative government or dictatorship	Global cooperation: institutions shaped by questions about the ownership and control of knowledge with supranational organizations/local governments the primary government units and participative democracy the norm
Paradigm	World viewed in purely natural terms	Knowledge base: mathematics (algebra, geometry), astronomy Central ideas: humans viewed as controlled by superior forces (i.e., God), religious, mystical outlook on life (astrology), and value system emphasizes harmony with nature	Knowledge base: physics, chemistry Central ideas: humans viewed in control of destiny in competitive world with belief that rational social structure can produce harmony by system of rewards and punishment	Knowledge base: quantum electronics, molecular biology, ecological sciences Central ideas: humans viewed as capable of continuous transformation and growth (whole-brain thinking); value system emphasizes autonomous individual in a decentralized society with feminine values dominant

ment will dramatically increase standards of living, free them from physical toil, and allow them to develop their human potential fully.

You should expect to benefit in at least four ways from this book. First, you should gain a clearer understanding of the broad direction that change is taking in the economy and society and the forces creating that change. Second, you should be able to use the change model to project and understand future changes. You should develop a sense of security when you see that change has a clear, predictable basis and direction that can be responded to rationally. Third, understanding the forces shaping your business environment should help you compete more effectively in your daily business life. Finally, you should make more effective investment decisions as a result of understanding the forces shaping the investment environment.

The Historical Evolution of the World's Economy

As you can see from the model in table 1.1, the world already has experienced two major shifts in its basic economic and social structure. In the first major phase of economic development, humans moved from a hunting and gathering tribal economy to an agricultural economy. This transition began approximately 8,000 years ago and is almost totally complete worldwide today with the exception of a few primitive societies in areas such as the Amazon Basin and New Guinea. In the second major phase, humans moved from an agricultural economy to an industrial economy. This phase began in Great Britain approximately 250 years ago and spread to Western Europe, North America, and Japan in the nineteenth century. Since World War II industrialization has spread extensively throughout Asia and portions of Latin America.

The third stage of man's economic and social history is the development of the knowledge economy and society. This process started in the United States approximately twenty-five years ago and currently is accelerating in both the United States and the rest of the advanced industrial world—Canada, Western Europe, and Japan. Its critical variables are information and knowledge.

To provide a perspective on this shift between economies, I will review the central characteristics of each. Of course, in a dynamic, real-world economy, elements of preindustrial, industrial, and knowledge economies may all be present simultaneously. We are looking at the dominant form of economy and the direction in which the economy is developing.

A preindustrial economy (which includes both primitive and agricultural economies) is an extractive economy. It is based on extracting a range of resources from the natural environment. The dominant economic activities of an extractive economy are farming, mining, fishing, and forestry. A society based on such an economy must be organized in a way that maximizes resource extraction; thus, economic and social organization is based on ownership of natural resources (predominantly land). In an extractive economy, you want to own the plantation or the mine.

Demographically, a preindustrial economy is very stable. Populations grow slowly or not at all. High birth rates are accompanied by high death rates, and average life spans are relatively short. In a primitive or agricultural society a lot of people are born, but few live to old age; there are many more young people than old. Because there are so few of them, the old are revered as a source of communal experience.

Although extractive activities and services may be part of an industrial economy as well, the machine production of goods is the central economic activity. Physical capital and unskilled labor are the major economic resources of an industrial society. Economic and social organization is thus based on financial and physical capital ownership. In an industrial economy, you want to own the steel mill or the automobile factory.

Demographically, industrial economies tend to be unstable. Societies in the early stages of industrialization tend to be characterized by rapidly growing populations. As industrial societies mature, population growth slows; the higher cost of bringing up children causes birth rates to drop. Falling birth rates are accompanied by even more rapidly falling death rates, as improvements in standards of living, sanitation, and health care extend the average life. In an industrial society fewer people are born than in a primitive or agricultural society, more live to old age, and young and old are more evenly balanced.

The knowledge economy differs from its two predecessors in that services, rather than goods production, provide the dominant source of employment. It is an information-processing economy in which computers and telecommunications are central and strategic because they produce and exchange the critical resources of information and knowledge. Scientific research and formal education are the basis of wealth creation. Economic and social organization is centered around the possession of information and knowledge and the utilization of human capital—that is, educated, skilled people. In a knowledge economy, you want to own the television station or the phone company.

Demographically, knowledge economies are initially unstable and then tend to stabilize. Better birth control techniques contribute to birth rates' falling sharply until they are at or below the replacement fertility rate. Population growth stops, and then total population begins to slowly decline. Few people are born, but most live to a ripe old age, creating a society with a lot of old people and few young people. In a knowledge society, we have fewer children and instead take care of our aging parents.

These three types of economy have one interesting thing in common. Through productivity improvements, each is able to maintain a higher standard of living and a more affluent population. An agricultural society is more affluent than a primitive society, an industrial society is more affluent than an agricultural society, and a knowledge society is the most affluent of all. Improvements in productivity are the prime economic movers in the shifts to new economies. This fact will be discussed in greater detail a little later in this chapter.

Knowledge: Definitions

In order to understand the critical differences between the industrial economy and the knowledge economy, you must understand what industry, service, and knowledge are. Webster's dictionary defines *industry* as "manufacturing in general" and *manufacturing* as "the production by hand or machinery of goods or wares, especially on large scale." It defines *service* as "work done for others which does not result in products or the supplying of some commodity, as water and gas, required by the public."

Webster's defines *knowledge* as "acquaintance with facts, truths, or principles from study or investigation; practical understanding of an art or skill; the sum of what is known or may be known." *Information,* which is often confused with knowledge, is defined as "news or intelligence communicated by word or in writing; facts or data." As this definition shows, information is the raw material of knowledge just as wood is the raw material of a table. A set of coordinates for a ship's position and a map of the ocean are information. The ability to use the coordinates and the map to plot a course for the ship from its current location to its destination is knowledge. The coordinates and the map are raw materials for plotting the course.

When you distinguish between information and knowledge, it is important to recognize that information can be found in a variety of inanimate objects from a book to a computer disk but that knowledge can be found only in human beings. Knowledge is understanding and expertise. Knowledge is the ability to apply information to specific work or performance. Only human beings can make such an application either through their brains or through their skilled hands. Information is useless without a knowledgeable human being to apply it to a productive purpose. A book that is not read is of no value to anyone.

Having just said that only human beings can have knowledge, I would like to qualify that statement. Computers started out simply as generators of information, but their current features could be defined as including knowledge. Even as they become increasingly sophisticated in their applications, however, computers still depend on human beings to program them and determine when to use them. Even more important, no one has been able to program a computer to make the connections between apparently unconnected information and knowledge, an ability that is the basis of creativity.

Knowledge can be considered a form of *capital,* for Webster's defines *capital* as "any form of wealth employed for the production of more wealth." It is common to think of a machine like an automobile assembly line as capital if it produces wealth. But physicians' skill and education produce wealth for them in the form of high income, so medical knowledge could be considered capital as well. Because acquiring a medical education is a major expense—classifiable as a capital investment—a doctor can be viewed as capital in human form, or *human capital.* This concept has been intuitively understood by the parents of generations of medical students.

Webster's defines *technology* as "the application of knowledge to work." Development of knowledge is thus a prerequisite to the development of technology. A faster rate of development of new knowledge lays the foundation for a faster rate of development of new technology. Table 1.1 shows that new knowledge leads to new technology, which creates economic change, which in turn leads to social change, which in turn leads to political and paradigm change. In the knowledge economy we create new knowledge at an accelerating rate, which results in the whole process of change being speeded up.

Knowledge: Characteristics

Four characteristics of knowledge and information make them unique resources and create a new economy:

1. Knowledge is expandable and self-generating. The raw goods of an industrial economy are finite resources; iron ore is used up as steel is manufactured. Unlike iron ore, however, knowledge increases as it is used. In using my knowledge to perform a task, I improve my knowledge and expand my understanding of the task. A surgeon who has performed an operation ten times has more knowledge and understanding of the operation than a surgeon who has performed it once. Thus in a knowledge economy, a scarcity of resources is replaced by an expansion of resources.

2. Knowledge is substitutable. It can and does replace land, labor, and capital. For example, a farmer who can grow more

food on a specific piece of land using new farming techniques does not need additional land to increase production.

3. Knowledge is transportable. In today's electronic society, knowledge moves at the speed of light. In a few seconds I can fax to Taiwan a schematic for a new computer chip that represents months of intensive engineering work.

4. Knowledge is shareable. The transfer of knowledge to other people does not prevent its use by the original holder. Sending a team of U.S. oil experts to the Soviet Union in September 1990 helped improve Soviet oil output but did not cost the United States any oil.

You and other individuals can acquire knowledge from a variety of sources—through professional and personal experiences, informally by reading newspapers, magazines, and books and watching television, and formally by attending courses at primary, secondary, and university-level educational institutions or on-the-job training programs. The knowledge economy differs from its predecessors in its emphasis on developing knowledge through formal research and development efforts and on transmitting abstract knowledge to individuals through formal education and training. In agricultural and industrial economies most knowledge was acquired through experience. People learned through doing. The son learned farming by following his father and the daughter learned how to make cloth by following the master weaver. In the knowledge economy people must learn basic subjects like reading and mathematics and advanced subjects like physics and accounting in the classroom before they can participate effectively in the knowledge economy.

For the full potential productivity of knowledge to be realized, it must be applied freely. For this reason totalitarian societies can never achieve the full economic potential of a knowledge economy. As the society with the broadest personal freedom and the greatest freedom of immigration, the United States is the laboratory in which most of the new economic and social structures of the knowledge economy are being tested and developed. The open U.S. system has no rival in unlocking the creative capabilities of its people.

Productivity: The Driving Force for Change

Productivity is the lever that moves economies from one level to the next. It can be defined as a measure of the amount of output—that is, goods and services—that can be produced with a given level of labor. Improvements in productivity allow a given level of work to be done by fewer people or more work to be done by the same number of people. From increased productivity comes more wealth. A fisherman who acquires a new net that allows him to double his catch per day is both more productive and more wealthy.

In our knowledge society increasing rates of productivity improvement are causing other changes as well. By definition, improvements in productivity free workers who must move to other work. A corollary of that rule is that the faster the rate of productivity increase and economic growth, the faster the rate of change (as more people must move to new jobs). In our new knowledge society an increase in the production and spread of knowledge results in an increased rate of technological change, which leads to increasing rates of productivity improvement.

When the U.S. economy shifted from an agricultural to an industrial society in the nineteenth century, the critical factor that fueled the transformation was improving productivity in agriculture. The farmer's ability to increase food production, so that fewer and fewer people were required in order to feed the population, allowed U.S. industry to develop. Improvements in agricultural productivity freed up farm workers to move to the city and participate in the industrialization process.

If agriculture had stayed at the levels of productivity that existed in 1750, the industrialization of the United States would never have occurred because the bulk of the population would have spent all its time trying to get enough to eat. The development in the late eighteenth and early nineteenth centuries of new farming technologies such as Eli Whitney's cotton gin and Cyrus McCormick's reaper, laid the foundation for the shift to an industrial society in the second half of the nineteenth century. When coupled with improvements in transportation (such as the Erie Canal and the early railroads) that improved the distribution of farm products, the new farm technology resulted in productivity gains.

The tools driving increased productivity in the new knowledge economy are computers, advanced telecommunications, robotics, biotechnology, materials sciences, laser technology, and energy technology. These new technologies enable farmers to produce more food with fewer people, manufacturers to produce better goods with fewer workhours and less material and energy, and a variety of service providers to provide more and better service with fewer people and less energy (see box).

Figure 1.1 shows a general model of how labor shifts from one sector to another over time as an economy evolves, and various categories of services grow and contract. Figure 1.2 shows how employment in the United States has shifted from agriculture to manufacturing to services over time.

KNOWLEDGE AND ENERGY USE

As the industrial economy grew, much more energy was used to run the economy and produce goods. When the price of oil went up in 1973, however, the advanced industrial countries of North America, Europe, and Japan were required to use less energy to produce the same or better goods if the existing standard of living was to be maintained or increased. Manufacturers had to use less energy through better technology. As a result, today's cars weigh less, houses are smaller, household appliances have fewer moving parts, and cars and airplanes go farther on a gallon of fuel. U.S. energy use and GNP growth moved in lockstep for fifty years up to 1973; since then additional increases in GNP have required less and less additional energy. While per capita incomes and living standards have improved, per capita consumption of energy has remained constant. In 1970 per capita annual consumption of energy in the United States was 326 million British Thermal Units (BTUs), and in 1988 it was 325 million BTUs.

Figure 1.1 How the Knowledge Economy Develops Through Shifting the Allocation of the Labor Force

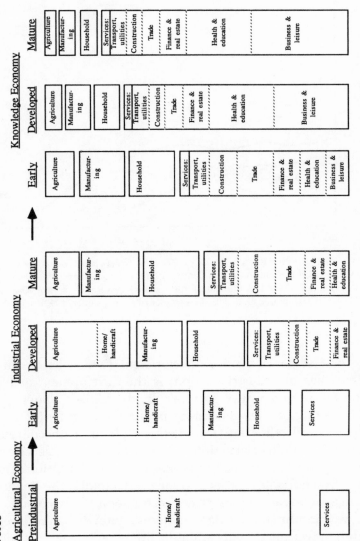

As productivity improves in a given sector (such as agriculture), fewer people are required to produce the output of that sector. People are free to do other work (such as in manufacturing), expanding that sector's employment until the market for the output of that sector is saturated.

Figure 1.2   U.S. Employment Trends from 1870 to 2000 (projected)

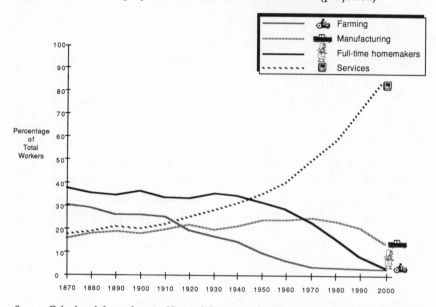

Sources: Calculated from data in *Historical Statistics of the United States, Colonial Times to 1970* (Washington, D.C.: U.S. Bureau of the Census, 1976); *Statistical Abstract of the United States, 1990* (Washington, D.C.: U.S. Bureau of the Census, 1990); and *Economic Report of the President, 1990* (Washington, D.C.: U.S. Government Printing Office, 1990).

The first stage of service development (which accompanies the first stage of industrialization) is the development of basic transportation and utility systems. In the United States giant railroads and electrical generating plants grew up beside major steel plants, oil refineries, and chemical plants in the development phase of industrialization. The second phase of service development follows the mature period of industrialization. Thus, when U.S. wholesale and retail trade grew rapidly, the financial, insurance, and real estate services sector soon followed suit. Finally, within the knowledge economy, knowledge services—including government, education, health care, business services, and leisure services—have quickly expanded. These services exist in both agriculture and industrial economies but grow rapidly only as an advanced industrial economy moves into a knowledge economy.

Innovation and Entrepreneurship: The Mechanism of Transition

How does an industrial economy become a knowledge economy? The driving force for the transition is increased productivity, but what causes these productivity increases? Innovations—new ideas in technology, organization, and management—are translated by entrepreneurs into more effective businesses, which in turn produce better products or services using less labor, material, or energy than do competing businesses. The ultimate effect of innovation is that less labor is required somewhere in the production chain of a product or service. Productivity improvements can directly reduce employment in both the more productive business and its suppliers.

The catalyst for innovation is profit. An entrepreneur will benefit from profits generated through innovation, and an existing business will benefit if innovation causes profits to increase. Both expect to profit, either by serving a new market or by serving an old market more efficiently and effectively than the competition—through higher productivity than the competition.

Thus the incentive of profit generates innovation, which in turn generates productivity improvement and change. In a socialist economy, by contrast, there is no motivation for innovation, so it is difficult to raise productivity. As the world moves toward knowledge economies, countries are increasingly turning to market economies because they automatically turn new knowledge into technological and economic innovation and improve productivity and living standards (see box).

The Characteristics of the Knowledge Economy

As the economy shifts from an industrial economy to a knowledge economy, it experiences a series of changes, including

- The automation of labor-intensive manufacturing activities, as well as increasing automation of a broad range of service activities;

THE INDUSTRIAL REVOLUTION AND PRODUCTIVITY

The fifty years from 1865 to 1915 was a period of unprecedented technological change. This technological explosion was documented by the U.S. Patent Office. In the 70 years from its creation in 1790 to the beginning of the Civil War in 1860, the patent office issued a total of 86,000 patents, or slightly more than 500 a year. Between 1860 and 1890 a patent explosion occurred as innovations transformed old processes in every industry and trade. During that 30-year period 440,000 patents were issued—an average of 14,667 per year, a rate of innovation and invention 30 times higher than that of the preceding 70 years. A major invention appeared on average every 15 months, creating hundreds of new industries.

Technologies developed during this period include the Bessemer steel process (the foundation of the steel industry), synthetic dyes (the foundation of the organic chemical industry), the Siemens electrical generator (the foundation of the electric power industry), the electric light bulb, the telephone, the typewriter, the photograph, the automobile, aluminum, and vulcanized rubber. The result was an explosion of productivity increases. Between 1870 and 1900 U.S. annual productivity growth (increases in annual output per worker) increased from 0.3 percent in 1870 to 1.8 percent in 1900, due to the rapid transformation of new technology into productive processes.

- The overall growth of service industries, with particular growth in health care, education, software production, and entertainment;
- The downsizing of major companies in both manufacturing and services, attended by an upsurge in entrepreneurship;
- A changing labor force, with a particularly dramatic increase in the participation of women (who are both the fastest-growing segment of the labor force and the most rapidly improving in terms of economic status);
- Substantial demographic changes caused by falling birthrates and an aging population;
- Shifts in the geographic center of the economy, from the location of raw materials and capital equipment to the loca-

tion of centers of information and knowledge, particularly educational and research centers.

One of the most dramatic aspects of the shift from the industrial to the knowledge economy is the speed with which the change occurs. Although the shift from an agricultural to an industrial economy in the advanced countries of Western Europe, North America, and Japan took several generations, the shift from the industrial economy to the knowledge economy is occurring within a single generation. Several key dimensions distinguish the knowledge economy from its predecessors, including the following:

- Basic scientific knowledge and research become the economy's driving force, generating new technology, providing opportunities for innovation, and creating new industries;
- Education plays a central role when knowledge services are the largest sector in the economy;
- Women increasingly participate in the paid workforce and seek complete pay equality with men;
- Ideology in politics declines, and economic and political power disperses;
- New management approaches to organizations are developed using computer technology and emphasizing human resource management.

Table 1.1 summarizes the central differences among agricultural, industrial, and knowledge societies in the framework of the economic change model.

Knowledge and Global Integration

This chapter has focused on the United States, but the shift to a knowledge economy is a worldwide phenomenon occurring in all advanced industrialized countries. Western Europe, Canada, and Japan are experiencing the phenomenon of deindustrialization as they move away from basic heavy industry and toward modern information technology manufacturing and information services businesses. As a result of this trend, the world economy has become more integrated, with more and more basic heavy industry based in Third World countries while the historically industrialized countries move into the advanced sectors.

Statistics back this up. It is estimated that by the year 2000 30 percent of all manufactured goods will be produced in Third World countries. This trend is particularly evident in the Pacific basin in the rapidly growing economies of Korea, Taiwan, Singapore, and Hong Kong. For the rest of the century, the Pacific basin, and in particular East Asia, will be the dominant area of world growth because of its heavy concentration of rapidly developing countries.

Along with the transition to the knowledge economy comes the collapse of what is known as *information float* throughout the world. Information float is the advantage that a country has in international trade as a result of developing new technology before other countries are able to develop or borrow that technology. Historically, the economic advantage of developing a new technology lasted a long time. England was able to dominate the world's economy for almost a century from 1815 to 1914 because it was the first to develop many of the basic technologies of the Industrial Revolution, such as the steam engine.

Today this form of technological domination is no longer possible. Modern computer and communication technologies (satellites, television, and telephones) have created powerful new systems for instantaneously transmitting information worldwide. If you saw the Olympics, transmitted live by satellite from Seoul; if you watched the live reporting from the Middle East after Iraq's invasion of Kuwait; or if you just watch the evening news regularly, you have experienced this technology. The result of this new worldwide communications network is that a technological advance is no longer a long-term advantage to the country that generates the advance. Within a few months of an improvement in personal computer technology by a U.S. firm like IBM, electronics firms in Taiwan, Hong Kong, or Korea have reverse engineered the technology and are making clones of the product for the world market.

The collapse of information float has led to the development of a transnational economy that transcends the controls and policies of individual nation states. This is most clearly seen in the advanced countries of Western Europe, North America, and Japan where the increasingly interlinked national economies have created a single economic market, termed *the Triad* by Kenichi Ohmae of McKinsey and Company. In the Triad information and knowledge flow freely through a number of mechanisms—business and tourist travel; students studying outside their home countries; corporations training employees in different countries; and corporations advertising to consumer markets in different countries. New ideas spread throughout the Triad very rapidly, so that none of the Triad countries maintains an advantage for long over the other Triad countries. Another result is that living standards and lifestyles grow increasingly similar throughout the Triad. Japanese enjoy Disney films and French wines, while Americans and Europeans delight in sushi bars and Honda motorcycles.

As the heads of the individual nation states in the Triad recognize their interdependence through increasingly close cooperation on economic matters, the political borders of the nation state have also begun to dissolve. You can see this clearly in Western Europe, where the European Economic Community will soon represent a single economic and political unit. But it is also evident in the increasingly close ties among the United States, Canada, and Mexico and in the continuing development of a variety of supranational organizations.

Multinational Corporations: The Agent of World Integration

Multinational corporations based in the Triad are playing a major role in this world integration. These organizations operate throughout the Triad and increasingly throughout the Third World, viewing the world as a single market. By implementing products and new technologies that succeed in one country in other countries, and by training workers and management in the various countries in which they have operations, multinationals are accelerating the spread of knowledge around the world.

ENGLISH: THE MECHANISM OF KNOWLEDGE DIFFUSION

The spread of knowledge requires technology to transport it and a common language to communicate the knowledge. Airplanes, television, and telecommunications are the current mechanisms for transporting knowledge, and English is the common language that communicates that knowledge. One billion people—over one-fifth of the world's population—are fluent in English either as a first or second language. The vast majority of scientific research is published first in English, the primary language of scientific communication. About 80 percent of the information stored in the world's computers is stored in English. The growth of English as the world's universal language is accelerating the spread of knowledge as more and more of the world's people, particularly the world's educated people, can communicate easily and directly with each other in this common tongue.

The auto industry provides a good example of how multinational corporations are creating a single world market. General Motors and Ford, as well as such major Japanese manufacturers as Toyota, Nissan, and Honda, have plants located on several continents and sell their products in most of the world's countries. The auto industry is now so globally integrated that automobile manufacturers talk about a world car. Similarly, consumer products ranging from Coca-Cola to Sony televisions, VCRs, and radios are manufactured on several continents and distributed throughout the world.

Although global markets are usually associated with manufactured goods, they exist in the service sector as well. If you are an affluent consumer in Europe and Japan, you carry the American Express card just like an American. If you are a traveling American, you can eat at McDonald's restaurants around the world from Paris to Moscow to Tokyo, or, alternatively, you can eat Kentucky Fried Chicken from London to Beijing. Citicorp is as well known by Asians and Europeans as it is by Americans.

One result of the spread of multinational corporations is that many major corporations are becoming "stateless"—making more sales outside their home markets than in their home markets, raising financing globally where money is cheapest, trading stock in New York, London, and Tokyo, and being run by senior management officials of many nationalities. Examples of stateless corporations include IBM, Citicorp, Nestlé, Volvo, Phillips, and Michelin (see box).

A second and more important result is that multinational corporations are creating a borderless world in which the nation-state is increasingly irrelevant to the economy. Companies organize around specific consumer markets without regard to national borders and locate their production or service facilities where they make the most economic sense rather than adhering to national development policies. As a result, the multinationals are accelerating the development of a world economy in which the prime competitive strength or weakness of countries is the quality of their workforce or human capital. The concept of human capital and its implications are examined in the chapter that follows.

2

Knowledge and People:
The Rise of Human
Capital

Compared to its predecessors the most characteristic dimension of a knowledge economy is the rise of human capital—that is, skilled, educated people—as the dominant force in the economy. Although the amount of physical and financial capital owned by an industrial society was critical to its success, in the knowledge economy physical capital decreases in relative importance as key elements such as the computer become cheaper and the quantity and quality of human capital increase in importance.

The Era of Human Capital

Human beings—their bodies, skills, and knowledge—are part of the capital stock of the world. Although it may sound very cold and inhuman to refer to people as capital, consider the popular business expression "The assets of this business go down in the elevator at night." In the computer industry, too, the primary cost of a new computer system is software, not hardware, and the quality and capability of that software is directly related to the ingenuity of the people developing it. In a knowledge economy the primary investment of a society has to be to upgrade the skills and talents of its people.

Japan is a classic example of an economy built on human capital. After World War II Japan's physical infrastructure was in ruins, and it had no valuable raw materials. Nevertheless, in less

24

than fifty years it has developed the most successful economy in the world. Its hard-working, highly educated population (Japan has the highest literacy rate in the world) has fueled tremendous growth.

A recent book—*Investment Markets* by Roger Ibbotson (professor of finance at Yale's School of Management) and Gary Brinson (president of First Chicago Investment Advisors)—calculates the percentage of the world's wealth in the form of human capital in 1984 and the change in the level of human capital in several leading industrial countries since the nineteenth century. Figure 2.1 summarizes those calculations. In 1846 human capital accounted for less than half of the wealth of Great Britain; by 1984 Ibbotson and Brinson calculate that 80 percent of the free world's wealth consisted of human capital.

Figure 2.1 Comparison of Shares of National Income Received by Human Capital and Physical/Financial Capital in Different Periods in Different Countries

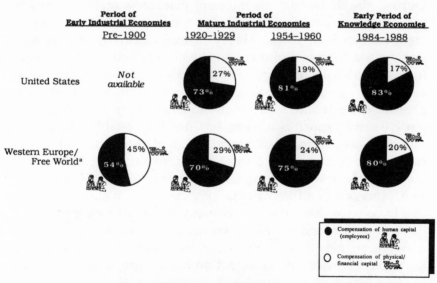

Sources: Simon Knuznets, *Modern Economic Growth* (New Haven: Yale University Press, 1966), 168–170; Roger Ibbotson and Gary Brinson, *Investment Markets* (New York: McGraw Hill, 1987), 21; and *Statistical Abstract of the United States 1990* (Washington, D.C.: U.S. Bureau of the Census, 1990).

[a]Pre-1900 share is average for Great Britain, France, and Germany.

1920–1929 and 1954–1960 is average for Britain, France, Germany, and Switzerland.

1984–1988 share is average for Western Europe, Japan, Hong Kong, Singapore, Australia, and Canada.

Another point made by Ibbotson and Brinson is that the value of human capital grows in the presence of increasing amounts of physical capital. Sophisticated machinery increases the value of sophisticated training and education: the highly trained nuclear engineer needs a nuclear plant to run just as the nuclear plant needs a trained staff to run it. In short, physical and financial capital adds value to human capital because it allows human capital to increase its productivity and to be more highly paid for professional skills. Similarly, human capital is essential to the production of physical capital: people invent new machines, construct new buildings, and create new businesses.

The Increasing Importance of the Knowledge Worker

During the Industrial Revolution machines replaced muscle power. In the evolving knowledge economy machines supplement human brainpower. Heavy manufacturing in the areas of steel, autos, rubber, and textiles is being replaced by knowledge-intensive high-technology manufacturing in such industries as aerospace, computers, telecommunications, home electronics, pharmaceuticals, and medical instruments and in knowledge-intensive services such as finance, broadcasting, health care, education, law, accounting, data processing, and entertainment. In the two decades between 1970 and 1990 approximately 90 percent of the new jobs created in the United States were in the information-processing and knowledge services areas. Figure 2.2 shows this long-term shift from an economy dominated by goods production to one dominated by knowledge services.

As more new jobs come from information-processing and knowledge services, the information worker (popularly called the white-collar worker) increases in importance relative to the total workforce. In 1960 the U.S. nonagricultural civilian workforce numbered 69.6 million people; by 1988 the civilian workforce had almost doubled to 115.0 million people. In 1960 the civilian workforce was composed of 47.1 percent white-collar workers, 39.7 percent blue-collar workers, and 13.2 percent service work-

Figure 2.2 Historical and Projected Employment in the United States by Major Economic Sectors

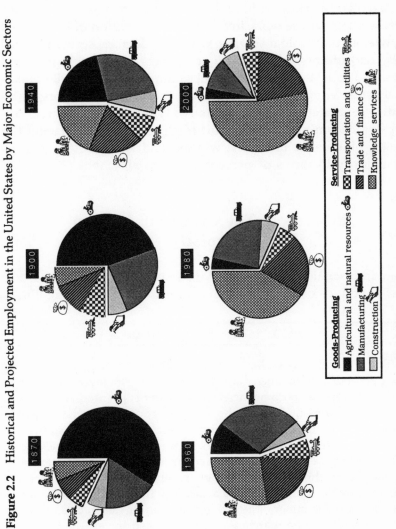

Sources: Historical Statistics of the United States, Colonial Times to 1970 (Washington, D.C.: U.S. Bureau of the Census, 1976) and *Statistical Abstract of the United States 1990* (Washington, D.C.: U.S. Bureau of the Census, 1990).

ers; in 1988 60.6 percent were white-collar workers, 27.7 percent blue-collar workers, and 11.7 percent service workers (see box).

Another development of the knowledge economy is the rise of the gold-collar worker. A subset of the more familiar category of white-collar worker, gold-collar workers are college-educated professionals whose work involves the application of specialized knowledge to problem solving. Lawyers, doctors, securities analysts, consultants, accountants, engineers, computer programmers, and college professors are all examples of gold-collar workers. Historically, these workers were too small a category to be treated separately by economists studying the labor force, but they are becoming the dominant form of worker, replacing the farmer, blue-collar industrial worker, and white-collar clerk as the majority in terms of percentage of employment.

Education: The Creator of Human Capital

In an industrial society education is available for limited and specific periods of time. Its main concerns are overcoming illiter-

---

KNOWLEDGE AND WARFARE

Since David slew Goliath, smarter warriors have been outwitting and outfighting bigger and stronger ones. However, in recent years warfare has become increasingly knowledge intensive as the technology and quality of the warriors count more than their quantity. Nowhere has this been more clearly demonstrated than in the Middle East. In three wars in the Middle East Israel has prevailed over the much larger forces of its antagonists because of its superior technology and the high quality of its soldiers, particularly its pilots. This was the U.S. strategy in its buildup in Saudi Arabia in the summer of 1990 after the Iraqi invasion of Kuwait. Rather than rely on matching the Iraqi armed forces, the United States combined a reasonably large force (but one significantly smaller than the total Iraqi military) with superior technology, intelligence, and communications.

---

acy and providing technical training. In the knowledge society education is universal and educational levels rise, for the new areas of knowledge require more training and updated education in order to be applied. College-educated technical and professional personnel become the largest occupational group.

You can see this transformation in the role of education in changing U.S. educational levels. At the start of World War II less than a quarter of the U.S. population over age twenty-five had completed high school, less than 5 percent had completed college, and the median amount of schooling completed by the adults over age twenty-five was 8.6 years. In essence, the average American in 1940 had a grade-school education. By 1988 over three-quarters of the U.S. population over age twenty-five had completed high school, more than 20 percent had completed college, and the median amount of schooling completed by adults over age twenty-five was 12.7 years. In less than fifty years average Americans had increased their education level from grade school to high school plus some college training. Among younger adults education levels were even higher and rising. In 1989 over one-quarter of twenty-two-year-olds completed college, over half of eighteen-year-olds started college, and over one-third of U.S. college students were older than twenty-five. In the future, the average American probably will be a college graduate.

In addition to formal education, Americans increasingly receive on-the-job training by their employers. Business plays a major role in human capital investment: its direct annual spending on worker training amounts to only slightly less than U.S. direct annual expenditures on higher education. IBM can correctly boast that it runs the largest educational system in the country.

The Growing U.S. Investment in Human Capital

Shifting to an economy in which human capital is the central resource creates a series of social problems. Historically, the private sector and its capital-financing mechanisms have underinvested in training, because they knew that workers could easily leave and take their training to a competitor. Similarly, workers have underinvested in education because they lose wages and possibly tuition costs while they pursue training. To guarantee adequate investment in human capital, governments in most countries have heavily subsidized education and training.

These higher levels of education and training of Americans reflect a massive investment in human capital on the part of the people, business, and the government, in the form of taxes, tuition payments, training expenses of business and government, charitable contributions to education, and direct living expenditures and foregone wages on the part of students. Forecasts for the 1990s predict that between one-half and three-quarters of all new jobs will require some college training because of the demands of modern technology.

In fact, the current U.S. annual investment in human capital substantially exceeds its annual investment in physical capital. In *The 1988 Economic Report of the President,* the President's Council of Economic Advisors calculated that in 1987 the United States invested approximately $610 billion in human capital and $440 billion in physical capital. This human capital investment was composed of $310 billion in direct annual expenditures on all forms of formal schooling (public and private primary, secondary and higher education, and vocational training); $100 billion in worker training by employers (exclusive of informal efforts to improve skills and performance on the job); and $200 billion in foregone wages of students age sixteen and over. By contrast, in 1950, at the beginning of the education of the baby boomers, the United States spent substantially more on physical capital than it did on human capital. Direct expenditures on formal education amounted to less than half the expenditures on new physical capital (compared to almost three-quarters in 1987), and both the amount of employer investment in worker training and the cost of foregone worker wages because of higher education were substantially less on a relative basis. Figure 2.3 shows how relative U.S. expenditures on human and physical capital have shifted since 1950.

Two factors will ensure that U.S. investment in human capital will continue to grow faster than investment in physical capital: (1) increased levels of higher education, both at the undergradu-

Figure 2.3 U.S. Investment in Human Capital Compared to U.S. Investment in Physical Capital, 1950 to 1989

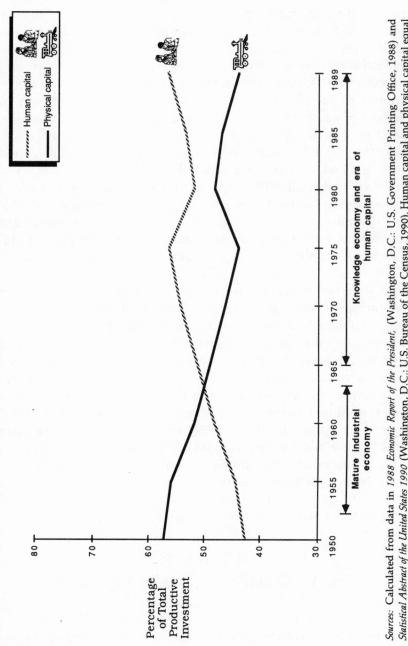

Sources: Calculated from data in *1988 Economic Report of the President*, (Washington, D.C.: U.S. Government Printing Office, 1988) and *Statistical Abstract of the United States 1990* (Washington, D.C.: U.S. Bureau of the Census, 1990). Human capital and physical capital equal 100 percent of productive investment.

ate and graduate levels, and increased formal training by business; and (2) increased governmental expenditures on primary and secondary education, and governmental and business expenditures on remedial education. Remedial education will be needed for the many citizens who are functionally illiterate and unable to participate fully in the evolving knowledge economy. Studies by the U.S. Census Bureau have shown that at least 10 percent of adult Americans read below the fourth-grade level or don't read at all. According to the United Nations Educational, Scientific, and Cultural Organization (UNESCO), the United States ranked 49th among 156 members of the United Nations in its rate of literacy in 1990. This ranking reflects a drop of eighteen places for the United States since countries were ranked in 1950.

This high rate of illiteracy in a society based on a knowledge economy is inextricably linked with many of the country's social ills. For example, studies have found that as many as three-quarters of repeat criminal offenders are functional illiterates, who often feel that crime is their only opportunity for economic advancement. Because of the high level of education in the general population and the increasing sophistication of military technology, even the volunteer military no longer accepts any recruit without a high school diploma. Thus the military no longer provides an avenue of opportunity for the poorly educated, as it did for many years. As highlighted in President Bush's 1989 education summit in Charlottesville, Virginia, a surge in state and local government programs in the 1990s is expected to improve basic education, while business is expected to expand its assistance to schools and educational programs within corporations. Increasingly businesses will realize that it is cheaper to educate and train their employees than to compete for employees from the limited pool of those with sufficient education.

The Worldwide Increase in Education Levels

The growth of investment in human capital is a worldwide phenomenon, with average levels of education rising in all developed countries. Japan, for example, graduated 23 percent of its twenty-two-year-olds from university in 1989 versus 26 percent in the United States, but a higher proportion of Japanese graduates received science or engineering degrees (26 percent versus 20 percent in the United States). In the critical areas of on-the-job worker training and apprentice programs, Japan and West Germany far exceed the United States in spending per employee.

Education levels are also rising in Third World countries, reflecting improved literacy rates worldwide and the transition of Third World countries from agricultural to industrial societies. At the end of World War II almost half the world's population and the vast majority of the populations of Asia and Africa were illiterate. By the early 1980s, however, for the first time in history, more than half the world's population age six to twenty-three was in school. By 1990 UNESCO estimated that only one-quarter of the world's adult population was illiterate and no continent had more than a 50 percent illiteracy rate.

The Changing Role of the University

Accompanying this increasing importance of education is a shift in the role of the university. In an industrial society the university functions as a social club and a training ground for members of the established social elite. A university education is a luxury and is not a prerequisite to obtaining decent jobs or even the highest positions in most areas of business and society. In the knowledge society, however, the university generates the scientific and technical research and new knowledge central to all aspects of the economy. A university education is a prerequisite to many jobs in the society and to advancement to senior leadership positions.

As a university education increases in importance, the number of colleges and universities and the number of teachers at those institutions also grow. In the United States there were fewer than 200 colleges and universities in 1900 but 3,600 by 1990; there were 10,000 college and university teachers in 1900, 110,000 in 1940, and 900,000 by 1990, reflecting the growth in size of universities since World War II. Before 1940 a university with more than 10,000 students was rare; by 1990 there were hundreds of universities with more than 10,000 students.

Research activities and knowledge production of universities also have escalated: by 1990 more than 40,000 separate academic journals in the sciences were publishing more than a million articles a year, or the equivalent of two new articles a minute. Although most of the articles do not contain scientific break-throughs, that level of technological and scientific research results in an acceleration of the rate at which basic scientific research is translated into practical applications.

As knowledge becomes the critical economic resource, universities, academic institutions, medical centers, and research corporations become centers of the production of human capital in the form of trained graduates and critical scientific information and knowledge. Rapid growth occurs in areas surrounding university towns as new companies and divisions of existing companies locate near them to draw on graduates and consulting faculty and to tap the knowledge created by university research activities. Examples include the area around Stanford University in Northern California (popularly known as Silicon Valley); the Boston area, which has a high concentration of universities and colleges (particularly Harvard University and the Massachusetts Institute of Technology); the Raleigh-Durham area in North Carolina (now known as Research Triangle); and Austin, Texas, which has drawn on the resources of the University of Texas.

The Half-Life of Knowledge and Lifelong Learning

Physical capital depreciates, and so does human capital. If you are over 40 like I am, you probably have discovered that the legs are the first thing to go. An awareness of the value of good health and physical fitness in our aging society has created a boom in the physical fitness industry—with growing support from employers. Business has begun to realize that it has a major investment in employees and that keeping those employees healthy and fit leads to higher productivity and lower health insurance bills.

However, the major problem of human capital depreciation is not the process of physical aging: it is the rapid obsolescence of knowledge and technology. As the development of new knowledge and new technology accelerates, it is harder for the experienced knowledge worker to keep up in his or her field. Engineering graduates are out of date within ten years of leaving school; physicians find that keeping up with new treatments, drugs, and technology is extremely difficult; accountants must attend continuing education courses; businesspeople have little time to learn about the latest computer technology or software programs.

The only way for knowledge workers to maintain their skills and knowledge and be effective human capital is to engage in lifelong learning, which will affect workers both as individuals and as employers and employees. In a society in which people return to school or retrain for new careers at middle age, occasional two-day seminars will be inadequate. Knowledge and technology are moving so fast that workers will need to return to school at frequent intervals throughout a career.

Electronics: The Technology of Human Capital

A knowledge society needs educated people to understand the information it produces, but it also requires technology to produce that information. This technology is produced by the electronics industry, which has grown into a $2-trillion-a-year industry worldwide dominated by the United States and Japan. In the ten-year period between 1972 and 1982 U.S. business purchases of high-tech equipment increased from one-quarter of U.S. business capital investment to one-half. The next chapter discusses the major technological advances that are transforming the world's industrial economies into knowledge economies.

3

Technology: Knowledge's Product

The world has entered a period of change that parallels the early stages of the Industrial Revolution. Based on a fundamentally new scientific infrastructure, the technology of the knowledge economy is radically different from that of the industrial economy. Industrial technology moved physical mass and created physical goods; the technology of the knowledge economy creates and moves information or, alternatively, reduces the physical mass of goods.

A classic example of the new technology's ability to rapidly move and manipulate information and reduce the physical mass of goods is fiberoptic cable. Fiberoptics replaces tons of copper wire with hair-thin strands of superclear glass to carry conversations, images, and data. Unlike copper wire, which uses electrical impulses, fiberoptic cable relies on light to transmit messages. Because of the characteristics of light, fiber optic strands can transmit 16,000 phone conversations simultaneously compared to the 24 capable of being carried by the equivalent length of copper wire. Using fiberoptic cable instead of copper wire enhances the ability to move information and reduces the demand for scarce material (copper), since glass is made from silicon (sand), a common material.

Technology's New Scientific Base

The technology of the Industrial Revolution was mechanical in nature and was based on Newtonian physics, developed in the seventeenth century. The technology of the knowledge economy rests on a host of twentieth-century scientific advances, particularly the advances in physics of Albert Einstein (whose work provides the foundation for modern nuclear physics), the mathematics breakthroughs of John von Neumann (whose work provides the foundation for computer technology), and the biological research of James Watson and Francis Crick (whose work on DNA provides the foundation for biotechnology).

We are all familiar with the technology of the knowledge economy. We think of it as high tech—computers, advanced communications, robotics, material sciences, biotechnology, lasers, and energy. This technology has dramatically affected productivity by allowing manufacturers to produce higher-quality goods with fewer workhours and material and energy inputs, and allowing service businesses to operate more efficiently with fewer people and material and energy resources.

Computers: Brainpower Multiplied

Central of all of the new technologies is computer technology. Until the development of the computer, all machinery was oriented toward assisting or replacing human muscle power. With the advent of the computer in 1945, routine human mental processes began to be performed by machine. As computers became faster and cheaper, the cost effectiveness of replacing routine human mental processes with computers expanded, and the use of computers spread.

Driving the growing use of computer technology have been significant reductions in the cost of computer technology. From 1945 to 1975 the cost of a relatively simple computer dropped by a factor of 100—from $10 million to $100,000. From 1975 to 1985 the cost of that same computer dropped again by a factor of 100—from $100,000 to $1,000—and from 1985 to 1995 it is projected that the cost of that same computer could drop by a factor of 1,000 (from $1,000 to $1). If the auto industry had experienced the same cost curve as the computer industry, you could buy a Rolls Royce for less than $1 and get more than 3 million miles on every gallon of gas.

Along with the dramatic drop in cost, increased use of the microcomputer, which was introduced by Apple in 1977, has fueled the growth in computer usage. In 1955 the world had only one installed general-purpose computer—the Eniac. The Eniac took up 15,000 square feet and weighed 30 tons, yet had less computing power than is currently available in a standard laptop personal computer. The next time you use a laptop computer, try and remember it once weighed thirty tons.

By 1990 over 50 million personal computers were in use in the United States with millions more used around the world. Declining cost, increased speed and power of hardware, and improved software have vastly broadened the range of applications for computer technology and enhanced its cost effectiveness, resulting in growing automation of U.S. manufacturing and wider use of computer technology in the service sector. Despite the cost decreases in computer technology from 1970 to 1985 as personal computers came into use, computers' share of U.S. business capital expenditures increased from 2 percent in 1970 to 19 percent in 1985. Computers should enable businesses to reduce material and labor costs in an extraordinary variety of ways. Computerized irrigation systems, for example, are expected to cut agricultural water usage in half (see box).

A unique characteristic of computer technology is its ability to generate new knowledge rapidly, which in turn speeds the development of new technology. The computer is the first machine to actively assist human workers in the generation of new knowledge, speeding up not only the process of new knowledge creation and technological change but also the process of the resulting economic, social, and political change.

Currently researchers in the field of computer technology are working toward the development of what has been termed *artificial intelligence*. Artificial intelligence is that part of computer science that is concerned with the design of intelligent computer systems—that is, systems that exhibit the characteristics as-

---

HIGH TECHNOLOGY COMES TO BROADWAY

Even Broadway is being reshaped by computer and communications technology. Andrew Lloyd Webber—the brightest star on Broadway, with three musical hits playing simultaneously—is no stranger to high technology. All his shows have used modern electronic technology, and *Cats* and *Phantom of the Opera* probably could not be produced without it. The prize for use of high technology in a Broadway production, however, should probably go to another Lloyd Webber hit, *Starlight Express.* Computers and fiberoptic communications were essential to this story of the great coast-to-coast train race. To run the lights, sound system, lasers, film projectors, and other aspects of the scenery, *Starlight Express* used six separate computer systems and twenty-two miles of fiberoptic cable. In addition to the basic computer systems, seven additional computers were used in the production as backups in case problems occurred with the basic systems.

---

sociated with advanced human intelligence, such as understanding language, learning, reasoning, and solving problems. In the first thirty years of computer applications, computer programs generally duplicated only the most routine of human mental functions. The development of artificial intelligence, coupled with the increasing power and low cost of computers, promises to be a particularly dramatic technological innovation (see box). The key to the expanded use of artificial intelligence is the

---

THE FINANCIAL EXPERT OF THE FUTURE

It is likely that much of the work associated with highly skilled jobs—those of lending officers or securities traders, for example—will ultimately be done by computer expert systems using artificial intelligence. American Express in the United States already uses an expert system to handle its credit authorizations for the American Express card. Sanwa Bank in Japan currently uses an expert system to select investments for its investment customers' portfolios. In the future, your friendly financial adviser probably will be a computer.

---

development of expert systems. Expert systems are programs that get the desired result—that is, they are intelligent assistants and advisers but are not intelligent in the human sense of exhibiting self-awareness and creativity. An expert system essentially has two parts. The first part is a set of rules that allows the program to make inferences and then explains to the user how it made them. These rules are created by a team of programmers skilled in knowledge engineering, who debrief human experts to learn the steps they use to solve a particular problem, and then capture those steps in computer code. The second part is knowledge about a specific content area. Programs that exhibit self-awareness and creativity remain a challenge for the future, as they require the replacement of logical reasoning in computers with human intuition and learning.

Communications: Brainpower Diffused

New communications technologies—including fiberoptics, communications satellites, long-distance microwave systems, cellular telephones, fax machines, video phones, and video cassette recorders—have made the world into the "global village" anticipated by Marshall McLuhan. Telecommunications is currently a trillion-dollar global industry: a billion telephones are in place, all interconnected and capable of directly dialing each other. In 1970, 23 million international calls originated in the United States annually; by 1987 the number had increased to 580 million.

As the world's communication system grows in size and volume of traffic, it also becomes more convenient to use. Mobile cellular phones (for both cars and personal carry) are expected to be a $30 billion industry by the year 2000, with 100 million cellular phones in use worldwide (versus the 180,000 in use shortly after the phones' introduction in 1983). New York City, which had 700 mobile phones in 1982, could eventually have as many as 250,000. The number of pocket pagers in use in the United States has also soared, tripling in the last decade. With the growth of beepers and voice mail, it is now possible to maintain communications when traveling even without mobile phones. Ultimately, mobile phones, beepers, and electronic voice mailboxes will be replaced by a personal telephone that can be carried everywhere. By the year 2000, a phone number will be a person, not a place.

Historically, personal telecommunication has been limited to voice communication, but that is changing. AT&T first demonstrated picture phones at the World's Fair in 1964, where they were a big hit. Commercial application started in 1982, with the opening of AT&T's first two video teleconference centers in Washington and New York. At that time, a one-hour conference session between New York and San Francisco cost $2,300 per hour. Currently, some corporations have picture-phone conference rooms in different cities, for use in intercity telephone conferences. Industry experts predict that by the year 2000 the cost of picture phones will have dropped to the point where they will be used in the home. In the future, you may worry as much about how you look as what you say when you answer the phone (see box).

The growth in telecommunications is being accompanied by growth in various forms of video communications, especially television. Home television is becoming a broad-based communication medium; with almost 60 percent of U.S. homes connected to cable today, specialized cable information services are an increasingly cost-effective way for business to communicate with niche markets. This use of cable is not limited to the United States. In Western Europe, France has approved a government

---

FAX MACHINES AND THE BEAUTY PARLOR

High technology has invaded the beauty parlor. In the summer of 1990 the *New York Times* reported a growing trend in the beauty and hair salons of New York and Los Angeles: customers bringing in laptop computers so that they could work while their hair was being styled. The article showed pictures of men and women typing away on their laptops while their hair was being cut or dried. According to the article, some beauty parlors had even installed fax machines so that customers could fax their work to clients or coworkers at the completion of their appointment. In the knowledge economy, your work is with you everywhere.

---

plan to connect most homes to cable by the year 2000, and West Germany and Great Britain's governments are promoting the expansion of cable throughout their countries. Soon television will be a 24-hour information medium capable of accessing a broad base of visual information and storing that information so it can be accessed at the viewer's convenience. Visual communication of information via the television will increasingly replace the printed word as the primary means of mass communication—a development that will revolutionize all aspects of the publishing industry.

Robotics: Brainpower Applied

Robotics, a new science based on the innovations of advanced computer technology, will be a significant factor in increasing productivity. Robots already are used in industry to perform a range of tasks, from painting to welding. Industrial automation also includes computer-based and computer-programmable controllers of industrial equipment, all of which enable manufacturers to increase quality control over their products while reducing costs through reduced direct labor and material costs and reduced waste. Robots will be staffing more and more factories as well as many service activities. A number of manufacturers already have developed or are developing robots for home use, while in the

---

THE POSTMAN IS A COMPUTER

The postal service has experimented with sending electronic messages to a receiving post office, where they are printed, enclosed in envelopes, and put in the regular mail stream. This may be the first step in developing an electronic-based information network for the entire United States and world community, in which government and private electronic mail systems are connected to corporate computer and information centers and to any home with cable television. Who will dogs bite when the postman is a television screen?

---

agricultural sector Australian engineers are developing a robot to shear sheep.

Biotechnology: Brave New World Revisited

Of all the new technologies, biotechnology offers the greatest potential for greater productivity and improvements in the quality of human life. The techniques of molecular and cellular manipulation, enzyme technology, microbial technology, genetic engineering, and bioprocess engineering all involve altering and manipulating the building blocks of life. Potential areas of application for biotechnology include agriculture (more productive plants and animals), health care (better drugs and vitamins), materials (biodegradable plastics and metal-leaching organisms for metal recovery), and manufacturing (biosensors). Some agricultural products expected to result from biotechnology include nitrogen-fixing crops that use sea water for irrigation, citrus fruits more resistant to frost, wheat that grows in the desert, soybeans immune to disease and insects, and rice that converts sunlight to energy with great efficiency. Beef cattle with strong immunity to disease, rapid growth rates, and an ability to eat inexpensive waste products will be produced through breeding techniques that use gene splitting. In this process, superior females are induced to produce eight to ten eggs instead of the normal one. After fertilization by a superior male, the eggs are implanted in an ordinary cow, which bears the calf. Through this technique one superior female could produce thirty to forty times its normal offspring.

Medical products expected to be made available through the advances of biotechnology include human insulin, interferon (which helps to direct the immune system), cancer antibodies, replacement genes, new drugs for the central nervous system to improve blood pressure, compounds that regulate calcium availability and thereby increase cardiac output, drugs that regulate the chemistry of the mind to be used in alleviating schizophrenia, anxiety, and depression, and miniaturized medical electronics for such items as cardiac pacemakers and hearing aids.

Materials: Strength from Sand

Material science, which often is overlooked in discussions of high tech, holds some of the greatest promise for improving productivity in the industrial sphere. As researchers are increasingly able to manipulate substances at the molecular level, new ceramics and plastics promise to reduce the cost and weight of a wide range of goods. Diamond coatings, ceramics, and reinforced plastics are greatly increasing the toughness, resilience, and useful life of many manufactured products by enormously extending the life of moving parts and surfaces exposed to wear, weather, and extreme conditions.

Ceramics (which are made from silicon, or sand) are now so strong that Ford Motor Co. uses ceramic tools to cut steel, and several prototype ceramic diesel engines can run without a cooling system, allowing higher efficiency and less weight. Similarly, high-strength polymers or plastics are being used for bridges, and plastic bumpers and fuel tanks will likely be common in new cars.

Lasers: The Miracle Light

Laser technology, still in its infancy, is considered by some experts to have potential equal to or greater than that of computer technology. *Lasers* (intense beams of concentrated light shining on a single wavelength) already are being used extensively in medicine, aviation, communications, heavy industry, retailing, and national defense. In medicine, lasers are used to perform delicate eye surgery, destroy cancerous tumors, and unclog diseased arteries. Prior to 1970 nearly all diabetics eventually went totally blind; today, laser surgery is able to save the sight of 65 percent. Similarly, while twenty years ago many kinds of brain and spinal tumors were inoperable, thousands of successful operations on these tumors are now being done with laser neurosurgery.

In aviation, new laser gyroscopes are used to navigate the Boeing 757 and 767 aircraft. In communications, lasers are central to fiberoptics. In heavy industry, laser cutting tools are being used to cut and weld steel. In retailing, supermarkets use lasers in the cash-register scanners that read the universal bar codes. And in the armed forces, lasers have a wide variety of applications, ranging from tank gun range finders and bomb targeting devices to communication systems for contacting nuclear submarines underwater.

Energy: Unlimited Power from Knowledge

Oil shortages in the 1970s stimulated the search for alternative energy sources. Since then other fossil fuels such as coal have received renewed emphasis, and untapped sources of oil such as shale in the Rocky Mountains and tar sands in Canada have been explored and developed. Even more significantly, alternative forms of energy that rely on continuous natural forces such as sun, wind, and water power have received increasing attention and investment. Windmills established in the California desert now provide electricity to the Los Angeles metropolitan area. Houses are heated by solar energy all over the United States, particularly in the Southwest. In Northern California—following the lead of Iceland, which receives most of its energy from geothermal sources—geothermal heat has been tapped as a source of steam to generate electricity. In Norway machinery harnesses wave power for energy, adding to the various sources of hydropower. This attention and investment guarantee that in the future more and more of the world's energy will derive from renewable natural sources.

For the twenty-first century, two areas of scientific advance hold out the promise of inexhaustible, cheap, and safe energy— nuclear fusion and superconductivity. In nuclear fusion additional fuel is created in the power-generation process, whereas today's nuclear fission process consumes its fuel. Since nuclear fusion uses as its energy source hydrogen (easily available from sea water) rather than the rare substance uranium, nuclear fusion promises to provide an inexhaustible supply of energy.

Superconductors are simply materials that can carry electricity without energy loss. The discovery of new superconductive materials in the late 1980s promises dramatic increases in efficiency in all aspects of electricity and would make feasible a range of technologies from electric cars to magnetic trains. More efficient electrical transmission systems also would make it possible to locate generating plants in remote areas thousands of miles from the population being served.

The Significance of Self-Generating Technological Change

One characteristic of all these technologies is speed of development. Because much new technology is involved in creating and spreading knowledge, the whole process is accelerating as technological innovation creates further innovation. Computers are now designing better computers. Self-generating technological change is at the heart of accelerated knowledge creation, technological change, and the resulting economic, social, and political change. The next chapter discusses how this technological change is restructuring the economy.

4

Restructuring: The Birth Pangs of the Knowledge Economy

Headlines in the daily newspapers today announce the turmoil occurring in the U.S. economy, from the mergers of major corporations (often through takeovers by corporate raiders) to the elimination of the jobs of middle managers in traditional industries. These headlines are symptomatic of a fundamental restructuring of the economy, involving the transition from a traditional industrial economy to a rapidly emerging knowledge economy.

Agriculture and Industry in Crisis: Global Overcapacity

As was discussed in earlier chapters, the transition from an agricultural economy to an industrial economy to a knowledge economy has been driven by ongoing technological change. Technological change improves productivity, and labor is free to move to new economic activities. The classic example of improved productivity is agriculture. In 1850 agriculture employed two-thirds of the labor force in the United States. By 1990 less than 3 percent of the U.S. labor force was employed in agriculture: most workers were performing other economic activities. Lower productivity on the farm in the Soviet Union (where 22 percent of the labor

47

force works in agriculture) and in China (60 percent of the labor force works in agriculture) is a major reason that the Communist giants cannot compete with the West economically.

U.S. agricultural productivity as measured in output per work-hour has increased over 600 percent since the beginning of World War II and continues to improve. Even though the country's population has doubled, employment in agriculture has dropped from a prewar 9.5 million to approximately 3 million today. If U.S. agriculture had shown no productivity improvement, it would employ approximately 20 million people today.

Even though U.S. manufacturing's productivity increases have been only half as large as those of agriculture, it too has experienced a relative shrinkage in its share of the workforce. Manufacturing employed 28 percent of the labor force in the United States in 1960 and twenty years later employed only 21 percent of the workforce. Dramatic increases in manufacturing productivity brought about by new computer and robotics technology could shrink manufacturing employment to approximately 12 percent of the workforce by the year 2000 and to less than five percent by 2010. This does not mean that the United States will stop manufacturing goods. Just as fewer farmers today produce more food than we can consume, a highly automated manufacturing sector will be able to produce all the goods we need but with a much smaller labor force.

One result of improved agricultural productivity throughout the advanced world has been the development of substantial overcapacity. The United States, Europe, and Japan subsidize farmers that are not needed from a purely economic perspective: the United States buys excess farm production; Europe has mountains of butter and cheese and lakes of wine in government storage; Japanese consumers pay outrageous prices for beef, fruit, and many other foods because the Japanese farmer is protected by high tariffs and quotas on cheaper imported foods. The total cost of farm subsidies in the Triad had been calculated to exceed $250 billion annually, which reflects an inability of farm labor in the Triad to move to other economic activities as rapidly as productivity improves on the farm.

Manufacturing has experienced similar overcapacity problems in basic industries like steel, chemicals, and automobile manufacturing as a result of productivity improvements and slow-growing or stagnant markets. In the decade of the 1980s this problem was highlighted by the rescue of Chrysler Corporation. As the knowledge economy continues to develop, large traditional companies in basic manufacturing sectors will decline, and many new, small innovative companies in the growth sectors of the economy—like computer software production and health care services—will flourish (see box).

Rapidity of change is another result of productivity increases. Both overcapacity and rapid change require organizations to be more responsive to their environment, resulting in mergers that consolidate industries with overcapacity and in downsizings as small size increasingly becomes a competitive advantage. As these consolidations and downsizings occur, the core of traditional industrial organizations—the middle manager—is increasingly being squeezed out and reemployed in much smaller companies or as self-employed entrepreneurs, reflecting the fact that most job creation in the new knowledge economy occurs in the small business sector. In the new knowledge economy small is beautiful.

During the period 1950 to 1970, at the height of the mature industrial society, job growth in the U.S. economy came princi-

---

THE KNOWLEDGE ECONOMY COMES TO EAST GERMANY

The merger of East Germany and West Germany in 1990 revealed how the transition to a knowledge economy affects labor. At the time of the merger, per capita incomes in East Germany were approximately 40 percent of the per capita incomes of West Germany. East Germany's percentages of employment in agriculture, manufacturing, and services were approximately the same as West Germany's were in 1970. Even though East Germany was the most productive country in the old Communist bloc, it was twenty years behind West Germany in terms of economic development. Because East German agriculture and industry were not competitive when the merger occurred, massive unemployment is predicted to occur as excess labor is moved out of agriculture and manufacturing.

---

pally from large organizations, including government. The economy created 20 million new jobs, and the *Fortune* 500 industrials accounted for over one-third of these new jobs. From 1970 to 1989 these trends sharply reversed themselves: the economy created 37 million new jobs, while the *Fortune* 500 industrial companies (which in the mid-1980s accounted for approximately 75 percent of U.S. manufacturing sales and 90 percent of total U.S. manufacturing profits) lost over 2 million jobs (see box). Over three-quarters of the new jobs were created by companies with fewer than one hundred employees, and nearly two-thirds were created by small firms with fewer than twenty employees concentrated in the service sector.

The driving force behind this employment reduction at the *Fortune* 500 industrials has been pressure for productivity and profit improvement. General Electric's experience in the early 1980s illustrates these forces. Between 1981 and 1985 Chairman Jack Welsh pushed GE through a painful struggle to improve productivity, investing heavily in machinery and automation and cutting GE's workforce by one-quarter—from 404,000 at the end of 1981 to 304,000 at the end of 1985. The resulting gain in productivity of about 4 percent per year was approximately four times the annual increase for U.S. business as a whole during the same period.

The restructuring of U.S. manufacturing has led one way of

TECHNOLOGY RESHAPES THE TRANSPORTATION SECTOR

The transportation sector (composed of air transportation, pipeline, railroad, water, and trucking services) accounts for almost 20 percent of the nation's gross national product. Freight and passenger transportation is being revolutionized by computer and automation technology, which is increasing productivity and improving safety. At the same time, fewer people are traveling as a result of electronic communications, and fewer goods are being shipped as the U.S. economy shifts toward a service economy, since services generally require less transportation than goods. Currently, transportation is the slowest-growing industry of the service sector.

---

work life to decline and a new one to rise. The United States and the other advanced industrial countries of Western Europe and Japan are producing high-technology goods and knowledge services for the world, as the less developed nations of the Third World take over basic labor-intensive manufacturing industries. For out-of-work U.S. industrial blue-collar workers and industrial middle managers new jobs will be waiting in small companies in service industries.

The Merger Game: The Mating of Dinosaurs

As the economy shifts from an industrial to a knowledge base, the excess capacity created in the manufacturing sector causes resources to be transferred to the service sector, where they can be more productive. Two mechanisms for this transfer are mergers of companies that seek to achieve economies of scale and eliminate duplicative capacity and divestitures of marginal operations by companies that downsize to become more efficient.

The late 1960s to the late 1980s was a period of intense merger and divestiture activity, with the mid-1980s being particularly active. Between 1968 and 1988 over 70,000 mergers and acquisitions were completed for a total market value of over $1.4 trillion. At the height of the merger boom in the mid-1980s, an average of eleven mergers were completed every working day. By late 1988 over half of the largest 1,000 U.S. corporations had undergone some type of significant reorganization in the 1980s. The largest volume of merger and acquisition activity occurred in the manufacturing and mining segments of the economy.

The Twilight of the Middle Manager

Blue-collar workers are not bearing the brunt of unemployment in the downsizing of major companies and the reduction in manufacturing employment. Job transformation and displacement occur just as frequently among office workers, clerical workers, and middle managers. Self-management is replacing staff managers as the span of control for senior management is widened and as computers increasingly are used to track and report departmental activity. Jobs like department heads, division directors, corporate engineers, corporate planners, human resource advisors, public relations advisors, finance managers, lawyers, and economists are being widely eliminated.

From 1979 to 1986 approximately half a million corporate managerial and professional jobs were eliminated in the United States. In the recession period of 1980 to 1982 approximately one-third of *Fortune*'s top 100 industrial companies cut their white-collar staffs. A wide range of industries was involved, including autos (General Motors, Ford, Chrysler, and AMC), natural resources (Exxon, Mobil, Texaco, and Alcoa), basic industry (Firestone and Crown Zellerbach), consumer goods (Levi Strauss), and high technology (Texas Instruments). *Fortune* 500 companies that cut staff in the 1980s estimate that between one-third and one-half of jobs eliminated were middle-management jobs. For example, at General Electric from 1981 to 1985 half of the 100,000 jobs eliminated by Jack Welch were middle-management jobs.

Small Is Beautiful

Many Americans dream of owning their own business and being their own boss, but in the mature industrial economy most were employed by large organizations and had few opportunities to find ways to express their entrepreneurial drive. Entrepreneurialism, however, has been the escape clause in the emerging knowledge economy. In the 1980s entrepreneurialism was the pressure-release valve in an economy that had less and less demand for middle managers. The economic impetus for the growth in self-employment was reinforced by deep demographic change. There just wasn't enough room for all the baby boomers who wanted to be executives. The number of persons thirty-five to forty-four years old (the prime years for entering middle management) increased by 42 percent between 1980 and 1990 while the number of jobs for middle managers was being slashed.

Before the industrialization of the late nineteenth century, all U.S. business was small business. Farmers, merchants, and skilled craftsmen all ran their businesses with a handful of employees or none at all. When industrialization led to the rise of large business organizations such as railroads, steel companies, oil companies, sugar processors, tobacco companies, and automobile companies, small business became the also-ran of American business. More and more people worked for large organizations, and big business increasingly dominated the landscape.

Over the last twenty years small business has begun to regain the importance it had before industrialization. The Small Business Administration defines *small business* as one with less than $10 million in assets and less than 500 employees. According to this definition, there were 19 million small businesses in the United States (corporations, partnerships, and sole proprietorships) in 1989—an increase of almost 50 percent since 1980, when the SBA reported 13 million small businesses. These 19 million small businesses employed 60 percent of the nation's labor force and accounted for half of the U.S. GNP. The U.S. small business sector represented an economy the size of Japan's.

This trend toward smaller firms is to be expected in a shift from a manufacturing to a knowledge economy: (1) less capital investment is needed to establish a company selling knowledge services, such as a law or accounting firm, than to establish a manufacturing plant; (2) the small entrepreneurial firm can move fast in a changing economy, since it lacks the decision-delaying bureaucracy of the large corporation; (3) the small firm has a natural product salesperson and champion in the entrepreneur, who has no vested interest in any established product line; and (4) the aging population characteristic of a knowledge economy buys fewer mass-produced durable goods and more personalized goods (like cottage industry crafts) and services from small firms.

One expert on economic change, MIT research scientist David Birch, contends that a fundamental shift is taking place in U.S. business as it is restructured from large-scale enterprises to smaller entrepreneurial and participatory units and from bureaucratic to entrepreneurial styles of management. Statistics show this trend: in 1950 approximately 93,000 new business started annually; by 1987 annual new business formations had increased 750 percent to 684,000. Accompanying the growth of new business formations has been a surge in venture capital. Between 1977 and 1982 new commitments to venture capital by established venture capital companies and institutions increased from $39 million to $1.4 billion as the entrepreneurial surge of the knowledge economy took hold.

Although the major source of entrepreneurial activity has been new companies in new industries, even successful big companies are restructuring themselves in order to be more entrepreneurial. Hewlett Packard, which has been one of the premier growth companies of the last ten years, has restructured itself into divisions of no more than 1,000 people to maintain the atmosphere of a small organization even in a multibillion dollar company with thousands and thousands of employees.

Jobs of the Future

All employment growth over the next ten to fifteen years will be in the service sector. Not all areas of the service sector will experience job growth, however—just those services associated with the development of the knowledge economy. Computer services, communications services, health care services, educational services, business services, and leisure services will experience increased employment and multiplication of the number of companies involved.

Expenditures in the health care sector by the year 2000 are predicted to be a larger percentage of GNP than the output of the manufacturing sector—an increase from 5 percent of the economy in 1960 to 15 percent by 2000. The city of Birmingham, Alabama, illustrates these trends. In 1967 Birmingham was the steel center of the Southeast, and U.S. Steel was Birmingham's largest employer with 30,000 employees. Today, U.S. Steel employs less than 4,000, and Birmingham's largest employer is the University of Alabama at Birmingham (whose principal activities are its Medical Center and health-related education and research) with over 10,000 employees.

Regional Economies Reshaped

As regional economies shift from industrial to knowledge economies, they are reshaped with great turbulence. Texas experienced problems as it moved away from an industrial oil-based economy to an economy based on services like health care and education. Another example of this regional restructuring is New England. In the early 1970s New England had a stagnant economy with traditional manufacturing industries (shoes and textiles) in decline due to high labor costs and foreign competition and unemployment substantially above the national average. More than 700,000 students attend 264 colleges and universities in the region, however, and by the 1980s New England was creating a new dynamic knowledge economy as its major educational institutions, led by the Massachusetts Institute of Technology and Harvard University, spawned a new generation of entrepreneurs who capitalized on the latest advances in science and technology. Major companies that emerged in New England included Digital Equipment Corporation, Wang Computers, and Lotus. Even more significant than major companies to New England's booming economy was an extremely strong base of small, entrepreneurial knowledge companies. In the 1970s almost 30 percent of U.S. new technology companies were started in Massachusetts even though the state had less than 3 percent of the U.S. population.

When New England shifted to a knowledge economy, it became the most affluent economic region in the United States with the lowest unemployment rate. New England's 12.5 million people enjoyed an average per capita income of $17,000 per year (17 percent above the national average) in 1987, and if New England were a separate country, it would have rivaled Switzerland as the wealthiest in the world (Massachusetts and Connecticut surpassed Switzerland in per capita income). Its unemployment rate stood at 3.7 percent, slightly more than half the national average. As a result of its transition, New England had some of the highest housing prices in the nation and experienced some of the greatest price increases even though its population growth has been minimal during the last ten years (between 1976 and 1986 the region's total population increased only 0.6 percent). The high housing prices directly reflected New England's knowledge economy affluence from both the high earnings of individuals and the increasing number of working women with the resulting growth of two-income families.

New England's experience as it shifted to a knowledge society followed the knowledge economy model with:

- The growth of service industries (between 1975 and 1986 total New England employment increased by 20 percent while manufacturing employment declined steadily);
- The primacy of basic scientific research and the dominance of universities (MIT and Harvard have led the boom, with Massachusetts producing more physics and engineering Ph.D.s per capita than any other state);
- High levels of education (New England has the best educated workforce in the country with the highest percentage of college graduates);
- Rapid growth of women in the workforce (60 percent of New England's women are in the workforce versus 55 percent nationally; in 1970 45 percent of women in New England ages 25 to 34 worked while fifteen years later 70 percent did);
- Changing demographics because of a declining birth rate (between 1975 and 1983 New England's labor force grew at half the national rate because of the baby bust of 1960s and 1970s).

In 1989 and 1990, however, New England entered a severe recession reflecting the excesses of its earlier boom. The hardest hit areas were banking and real estate, reflecting both speculative excesses and the general shrinkage in banking and real estate that occurs as the knowledge economy matures. As static population growth reduces the demand for new housing and commercial property, the real estate sector and banking sector (which depends heavily on real estate finance) shrink. This phenomenon is discussed in greater detail in the third section of the book.

Despite its recession New England still maintains some benefits from its earlier transition. For example, preliminary returns of the 1990 U.S. Census confirm that Connecticut still enjoys the highest per capita income of any state. New England should enjoy a prosperous, stable economy once it has worked out its over-capacity in the real estate and banking areas.

California: Laboratory for the Future

If you want to see the world's future, visit California. For many years, California has been recognized as the trend-setting state for the United States, but it also is trend setter for the world. It has the world's most dynamic knowledge economy coupled with a large and steady immigration from Third World countries. Asians, Africans, and Latin Americans are streaming into California, as a visit to Los Angeles International Airport readily shows.

Adding to California's role as the world's laboratory for the future is its open society, which has been known for decades for its ability to absorb and provide opportunities for newcomers. It has been a state where dreams flourish and capabilities count for more than connections. How California absorbs the current stream of immigrants, most of whom are not highly skilled, may indicate how the knowledge economy eventually might spread from countries in the Triad to the Third World.

California's growth is fueled by its position as the center of research and development of high technology in the United States. It is home to some of the country's leading research universities, including Stanford, the University of California at Berkeley, the University of California at San Diego, and the California Institute of Technology. Indeed, many of the most promising fields of new technology are dominated by California companies, including semiconductors, microcomputers, genetic engineering, laser technology, video communications, and the commercial exploitation of outer space. Through this base of high technology, California created almost a third of the nation's new jobs in the 1980s (see box).

California's advantage in high-technology industries has been its well-educated and highly skilled labor force. For years California's labor force has been high quality and technically skilled with twice the national average in percentage of college graduates in the adult population and over one-third of the nation's computer engineers. Added to California's human capital is an entre-

---

CALIFORNIA: AN ECONOMIC SUPERPOWER

If California were a separate nation, its economy would make it the eighth-largest country in the world in terms of GNP and put it substantially ahead of countries such as China with populations forty times larger. The only countries with economies larger than California's are the United States, Japan, the Soviet Union, West Germany, France, Italy, and Britain. By the year 2000 California should pass Italy and Britain and may pass France to become the fifth or sixth largest. In the decade 1980 to 1990 California added 6 million people to a total of 30 million and is expected to add a total of 10 million more by the year 2010. In the decade 1980 to 1990 California increased employment by 25 percent and its share of total jobs in the United States to 12 percent.

---

preneurial spirit flowing from its historically open society. Santa Clara County, the home of "Silicon Valley," is a hotbed of small, high-technology companies and related small service companies that have made it one of the country's fastest-growing areas over the last twenty years. Over 90 percent of Santa Clara's companies have fewer than 100 workers. Of high-technology manufacturing companies in Santa Clara, 80 percent have fewer than 200 workers.

Currently, California is the state experiencing the greatest amount of immigration, and because this immigration is predominantly from Third World countries, it is estimated that by the year 2000 whites will no longer constitute a majority of the population. By that time, California will truly represent a broad multiracial society, having changed in thirty years from a population 90 percent white to one in which whites are a minority.

5

Society Reshaped: Social and Demographic Change

Gender-limited social roles in the United States have changed dramatically since Betty Friedan wrote her famous book *The Feminine Mystique* in 1963. Whether measured by education levels, participation in the workforce, family size, or divorce rate and singlehood, the experience of young Americans has been dramatically different from that of their parents. Role changes for men and women are part of the continuing evolution of human society. They typically occur as societies shift from an agricultural to an industrial society or from an industrial to a knowledge economy.

The Historical Pattern of Social Change

In the shift from an agricultural to an industrial economy, the extended family loses its economic significance, and small families with a father as provider and a mother as caregiver predominate. Then, in the shift to a knowledge society, this nuclear family dissolves. Society becomes centered around the individual; tasks are no longer assigned by gender. Education, marketable skills, and paid employment allow women to attain financial independence, which, in turn, results in a dramatic reshaping of society as women gain greater power in both the family and society.

Before industrialization men and women worked side by side at necessary tasks, and society was structured around the family. Households were separate, self-sufficient economic units in which domestic and economic activities mingled, and each household contributed to its community on a cooperative basis. The first factories to emerge in England thus employed entire middle-class and lower-class families, including men, women, and children. With the establishment of child-labor laws in the mid-1800s, however, many women returned home to care for their children, and home and workplace became increasingly segregated by sex. Most women did not work outside the home, while working women clustered in "women's jobs" such as sewing, child care, and teaching.

During World War I and World War II many U.S. women worked at jobs left by servicemen. Between 1939 and 1943 three-quarters of the U.S. civilian labor force was married women, the majority of whom had children. After the war most of the younger women left the workforce to have families, while most of those over forty-five stayed in the labor force. During the baby boom from 1946 to 1962 the growth in labor force participation took place almost entirely among older women with grown children.

After 1962, as the birth rate declined because of widespread use of the birth control pill, younger women increasingly viewed work positively, and found work not only in traditionally female fields such as education and personal services but also in many fields that were newly opened to women. Of the 25 million increase in the number of women in the female labor force from 1947 to 1978, 40 percent resulted from growth of the general population and 60 percent from the increased participation of women. Evolving social attitudes resulted in major new federal and state laws in the 1960s and early 1970s designed to expand women's employment and educational opportunities, including the Equal Pay Act of 1963, Title VII of the Civil Rights Act of 1964 (which established the Equal Employment Opportunity Commission), Executive Orders 11375 and 11478 of 1967 (which

established affirmative action programs), the Education Amend-
ments of 1972, the Women's Educational Equity Act of 1974, the
Equal Credit Act of 1974, and the addition of equal rights amend-
ments to sixteen state constitutions. By the end of the 1970s, a
widespread change in women's attitudes toward work had occurred. In 1967, 60 percent of women agreed that a woman's place
was in the home; in 1977, 25 percent felt that way. By 1980, only
16 percent of women under age twenty-five planned to be housewives and did not desire a career.

Technology and Social Change

Technology drives the economic and social changes that accompany the shift to the knowledge society. Automatic dishwashers,
microwave ovens, and other products eliminate many tasks for-
merly associated with keeping a home. Birth control technologies
allow women to control the size of their families to a greater
extent than ever before. In the workplace computers reduce the
differences between the capacities of men and women and increase the value of women's labor.

The importance of the women's movement of the 1960s and
1970s as a catalyst for changed social attitudes about men's and
women's roles cannot be underestimated. It is doubtful, however,
that the dramatic change in sex roles and expectations that has
occurred over the last twenty-five years would have been possible without the technological changes that supported it.

Betty Friedan's Harvest: The Emergence of Women

You can see the dramatic shift in men's and women's experience
in the last twenty-five years by looking at education. In 1950
female students made up 30 percent of college enrollment; by
1980 they represented 52 percent of college students. In 1950
female college students overwhelmingly were enrolled either in
the liberal arts to prepare them for being homemakers or in edu-

cation to prepare for the traditionally female-dominated professions of teaching and nursing. About 1970 a revolution in women's expectations occurred, and young women increasingly sought education in the full range of professional disciplines in preparation for careers similar to men's. For example, between 1972 and 1985, women increased their share of accounting degrees awarded from 11 to 46 percent, MBAs awarded from 5 to 35 percent, law degrees awarded from 5 to 35 percent, medical degrees from 12 to 33 percent, and of doctorates awarded from 14 to 37 percent (see box).

Equally dramatic has been women's increased participation in the workforce. In 1950 only one-third of all women between the ages of twenty and sixty-four were in the paid workforce; by 1990 the percentage had more than doubled to over two-thirds, with the greatest increases among women with school-age children. At the beginning of World War II less than 10 percent of women with children under age eighteen were in the workforce;

A SPECIAL ANNIVERSARY

In 1990 the University of Virginia celebrated a milestone in its history. Founded by Thomas Jefferson in 1819, U. Va. was known for most of its history as the leading university for training "Southern gentlemen." For 150 years Virginia's students traveled great distances for female companionship. In 1970 Virginia started to admit women on a regular basis into its freshman class: 1990 marked twenty years of coeducation at Virginia. Visiting the campus of U. Va. (or "grounds" as students and alumni call it) in 1990, there is little evidence that the university was all male for most of its existence.

Young women are in fact a slight majority of the student population. In the 1960s, a young man could lose his prize possession of a room on "the Lawn" in buildings designed by Thomas Jefferson for having a woman visitor in the room. When I returned as an alumnus in the early 1970s, young women lived on "the Lawn." Whether going to class, playing rugby, or marching in ROTC, U. Va.'s young women of 1990 share the same experiences as its young men.

by 1980 the majority of women with children under eighteen were in the work force.

The norm has shifted as a direct result of technologies that have simplified housekeeping and of higher educational levels that have made economic opportunities available to women. The fact that women without a college degree are three times as likely to interrupt their careers for a family as those with a college degree confirms this. Figure 5.1 shows the changing participation rate of women in the U.S. paid workforce since 1870 and contrasts it with the participation rate of men.

Changing Expectations of Men and Women

As the educational and work situations of women change, society's expectations of them are changing as well. Women are increasingly occupying positions of leadership and assuming the characteristics associated with male styles of leadership—becoming more independent, decisive, and goal-oriented through early conditioning, diversification of role models, education, broadened opportunity, and lifestyle modifications. Similarly, young men experience women in positions of power and authority in all aspects of life and compete directly with women in school and on the job throughout their lives. This change in gender roles has been particularly painful for some Americans born before 1950 who have had to redefine their expectations about work, marriage, and family.

By the year 2000 virtually all women will be employed for part if not all of their adult lives. Accompanying this change in employment status are tremendous changes in role modeling, parenting, and basic formative experiences concerning gender. In the future there will be more role diversification, and sex will not be the dividing line of opportunity (see box).

Women in male-dominated cultures often have been socialized to feel responsible for the emotional needs of others—particularly husbands and children—before their own. In the future, the average woman will be far more self-reliant. She will be able to

Figure 5.1　U.S. Labor Force Participation Rates by Sex, 1870–1990 (percentage)

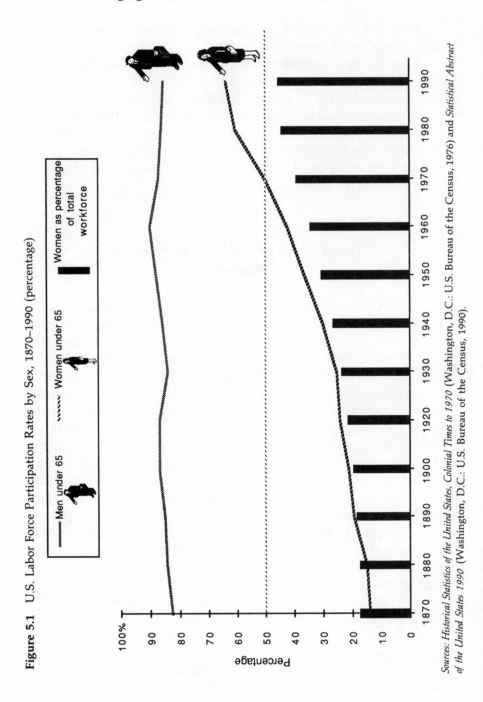

Sources: *Historical Statistics of the United States, Colonial Times to 1970* (Washington, D.C.: U.S. Bureau of the Census, 1976) and *Statistical Abstract of the United States 1990* (Washington, D.C.: U.S. Bureau of the Census, 1990).

"MOM'S WAR"

The buildup of U.S. armed forces in Saudi Arabia in August of 1990 provided the military with an opportunity to display how it would respond to changes in the U.S. labor force. Eleven percent of the armed forces are women, and many are married with children. For the first time in its history the United States sent mothers to war. Mothers (and even grandmothers) said goodbye to their children as they left with their units for Saudi Arabia and the risk of potential combat.

Once in Saudi Arabia women filled a wide range of positions from nurses to helicopter pilots for the 101st Airborne (one of the army's elite combat units) and tank mechanics for the 24th Mechanized Division. In contrast to these dramatic new roles for women Iraq's leader Saddam Hussein released Western women and children (the traditional noncombatants) and initially kept Western men as hostages and human shields.

---

give and to receive and will not do things that other people are capable of doing for themselves. Surveys in the 1980s showed that the vast majority of young American women expected to combine a career, marriage, and children.

The new measurement for a woman's status is not her competence as a wife and mother but her competence as a person. Compliance and deference to fathers and husbands are being replaced by competence, intelligence, achievement, and compassionate strength.

Examining why women work offers insight about the major forces reshaping society in the knowledge economy. Almost all women work primarily for one of two reasons—money and self-fulfillment. For many women the internal rewards of a job are as great as or greater than the value of a paycheck. A survey from the late 1970s showed that half of all women who worked full-time worked mainly for income, while half were motivated primarily by the need for self-respect and by the intrinsic interest of the job. For these women, the job provided fulfillment and self-actualization.

The Family Redefined

Higher education, work experience, changing attitudes about gender, and greater economic freedom for women has led to major changes in family structure and marriage. Marriages are shorter and serial, and attitudes and expectations about intimate relationships have changed. Men and women marry later, do not marry at all, live alone, live together outside marriage, and frequently dissolve marriages. In 1950 the median age at which women married was 20.3 years; this increased to 23.3 years by 1985. In 1950 one in six marriages ended in divorce; by 1980 the rate was one in two. The U.S. Census Bureau shows that for men and women born between 1946 and 1956 60 percent of first marriages will end in divorce.

Higher levels of economic self-sufficiency and self-orientation have led to attitudes supporting greater acceptance of an independent female lifestyle. A survey in 1957 found that 80 percent of Americans were severely critical of singles and none valued it as a lifestyle; in 1978 only 25 percent were critical and 14 percent valued the single lifestyle, with the overall majority being neutral. Similarly, in 1967 a survey of parents of college students found that 85 percent opposed premarital sex; by 1979 63 percent of those surveyed condoned premarital sex.

Parenting is undergoing a major transformation, a change that is dramatically affecting men, women, and children. Biological motherhood and parenting are becoming separate functions, with the parenting role being split and assumed by a combination of father, mother, and parental surrogates of both sexes, like day-care personnel. The perception of affordable, quality child care as a social necessity, not a private luxury, is growing, and there is an increasingly wide variety of day-care situations, ranging from in-home cooperatives shared by groups of parents to on-the-job, employer-provided facilities to government-sponsored programs.

The concept of the family is being revised to include many kinds of living arrangements. For example, the number of rotational families—in which no single, stable cast of characters lives together for a lifetime but a series of individual males and females share quarters—is beginning to surpass the number of nuclear families. In the future, families may no longer be defined as a "group of persons of common ancestry." By 1980 women headed 25 percent of all U.S. households, and only 7 percent of all U.S. families had fathers who worked outside the home and mothers who devoted themselves exclusively to the care of children. By the year 2000 it is projected that only 53 percent of all households will be composed of married couples, with the balance being composed of single-parent families (15.1 percent) and nonfamily households (31.8 percent).

The Unexpected Consequence: Baby Bust and an Aging Society

At the same time that marriages have been deferred and dissolved, bearing children has been deferred or decided against. Birth control and abortion now offer women more control over the maternal role, and women who choose to have children wait longer after marriage to do so. Accompanying the decline in marriage and in women's interest in child rearing is a decline in the birthrate, which frees women from the caretaker role and permits more time to work outside the home.

In 1960 only 24 percent of all young married women age twenty to twenty-four were childless. By 1978 this figure was 41 percent. In the period 1955 to 1959 the fertility rate (that is, the number of children the average woman will bear over her lifetime) in the United States for women in their childbearing years averaged 3.7 children per woman. By 1985 this rate had dropped over 50 percent to 1.6 children per woman in her childbearing years. Average family size in the United States has declined from 2.44 children per family in 1945 to 1.85 in 1965 (see box).

This reduction in the fertility rate is a deliberate choice. A survey in 1980 of U.S. women under thirty showed 23 percent wanted one or no children, 72 percent wanted a maximum of three, and only 5 percent wanted four or more. This reduction in the birthrate has been accomplished through a combination of birth control (such as contraceptive pills, diaphragms, and con-

---

"I WANT A CHILD"

In an August 1990 cover story in *People* magazine, television newswoman Connie Chung was quoted as saying, "I want a child." The article reported how Chung was one of many well-known women who either had borne their first child after they were forty or were trying to. The article told how singer Bette Midler, actress Ursula Andress, actress Glenn Close, and newswoman Mary Alice Williams had all given birth to their first child after age forty. According to the article, women who delay having children in order to have a career are creating a golden age for fertility medicine.

---

doms) and abortion. Since the mid-1970s there has been one abortion in the United States for every two live births.

Dropping birthrates and longer life expectancies due to medical advances also are causing major changes in the age structure of the United States. Since 1900 average life expectancy in the United States has increased twenty-six years. In 1970 the median age in the United States was twenty-eight and the population over age sixty-five was 21.1 million. In 1983 persons sixty-five and older outnumbered teenagers for the first time. By 1985 the median age had increased to thirty-one and the over sixty-five population was 28.6 million, equal to about 12 percent or one in eight of all Americans. Both will steadily increase. By 2020 the median age is expected to rise to thirty-nine and the over sixty-five population to grow to 45 million or one in five Americans.

The changing age structure is affecting all age groups. For example, the fastest-growing segment of the population by 1985 was the eighty-five and over category. The number of Americans over age eighty-five will grow from 2.4 million in 1980 to 5.1 million in 2000 for an overall increase of over 100 percent. Similarly, there will be a dramatic increase in the nation's middle-aged population (defined as age thirty-five to sixty-four), which will increase from 73 million in 1980 to 105 million in the year 2000. Figure 5.2 compares and contrasts the falling fertility rate in the United States since 1820 with the rising median age of the U.S. population over the same period of time. Figure 5.3 shows the

Figure 5.2 U.S. Fertility Rates and Median Ages, 1820–2020

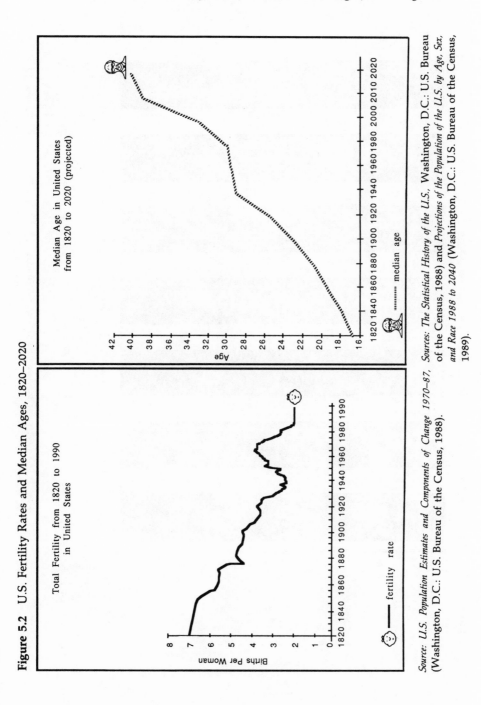

Total Fertility from 1820 to 1990
in United States

Median Age in United States
from 1820 to 2020 (projected)

—— fertility rate

·········· median age

Source: U.S. Population Estimates and Components of Change 1970–87, (Washington, D.C.: U.S. Bureau of the Census, 1988).

Sources: The Statistical History of the U.S., Washington, D.C.: U.S. Bureau of the Census, 1988) and *Projections of the Population of the U.S. by Age, Sex, and Race 1988 to 2040* (Washington, D.C.: U.S. Bureau of the Census, 1989).

Figure 5.3   U.S. Population, by Age Groups, Actual and Projected, 1960–2020

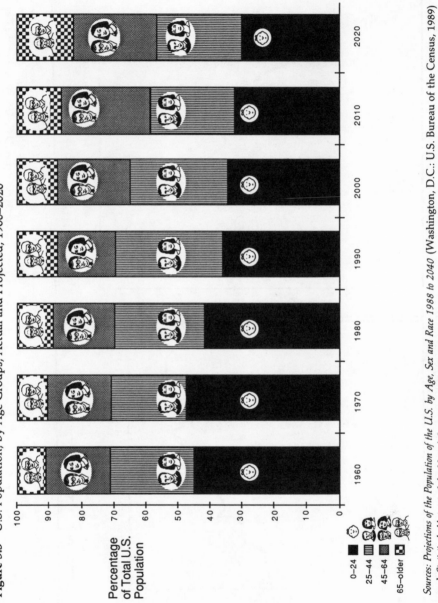

Sources: Projections of the Population of the U.S. by Age, Sex and Race 1988 to 2040 (Washington, D.C.: U.S. Bureau of the Census, 1989) and Statistical Abstract of the United States 1989 (Washington, D.C.: U.S. Bureau of the Census, 1989).

changing percentages of the U.S. population in different age groups for the period 1960 to 2020.

The low U.S. birth rate causes a rising median age and would normally lead to a declining population because the birth rate is below the replacement rate. Unlike other countries experiencing low birth rates, however, the United States has ongoing and massive immigration. Legal immigration into the United States amounts to 600,000 people a year, and illegal immigration is estimated at 1 to 2 million people a year, resulting in continuing population growth. But the baby bust is causing U.S. population growth to slow. In the decade 1990 to 2000 there will be an additional increase in population of 7.3 percent, with the U.S. population reaching 268 million by the year 2000. This represents a growth rate of less than 1 percent a year. The United States should reach zero population growth in the year 2050 at an over-all total of 309 million persons.

Global Demographic Change

A dramatic reduction in fertility rates over the last twenty-five years is not unique to the United States. All the advanced countries of the Triad (the United States, Canada, Western Europe, and Japan) have experienced substantial reductions in fertility rates since 1950. Currently, all Triad countries except for Ireland have fertility rates below the replacement rate of 2.1 children per woman, and Ireland is at the replacement rate of 2.1. Many major countries have lower fertility rates than the United States. Germany and Italy, for example, have fertility rates of 1.4, and Japan has a fertility rate of 1.57. The EEC as a whole has a fertility rate of 1.58. For much of the twentieth century the world has worried about German militarism, but with its current fertility rates Germany won't have enough young people to field a significant army in the twenty-first century.

Because the other Triad countries (with the exception of Canada) do not have significant immigration, the aging of their populations will be even more dramatic than the aging of the U.S. population. Currently, the EEC's percentage of its population over age sixty-five is higher than the United States' (14 percent versus 12 percent), and the gap should widen due to the EEC's lower fertility rate and its low levels of immigration. Japan currently has an even higher percentage of its population over sixty-five than the United States and Europe, with one in eight Japanese over sixty-five. By the year 2020 one in four Japanese will be over sixty-five, which should be the highest percentage of elderly in any population in the Triad.

In the Third World fertility rates have been falling too. Between 1960 and 1990 UN data show sharp declines in fertility rates in much of the Third World. China's fertility rate fell from 5.9 to 2.4, India's from 5.8 to 4.3, Indonesia's from 5.4 to 3.3, and South Korea's from 5.4 to 2.0. Brazil's fertility rate fell from 6.1 to 3.5 and Mexico's from 6.8 to 3.6. These declines mirror the dropping fertility rates that accompanied the industrialization of the advanced countries of Western Europe, North America, and Japan and reflect the industrialization of the Third World. As would be expected, these declining fertility rates in the Third World are being accompanied by rising median ages. In the future, as current Third World countries shift to knowledge economies, their fertility rates should match those that the countries in the Triad are currently experiencing.

The Economic Effect of Demographic Change

The social and demographic changes that accompany the transition to the knowledge economy have profound economic consequences. Since about 1985 the United States has experienced labor shortages as fewer young people enter the labor market, and these shortages will increase substantially in the 1990s. Similarly, the massive entry of women into the workforce in the United States is creating new markets for services such as day care centers and restaurants. Internationally, the growing elderly population of Europe and Japan relative to the United States will increasingly hurt their economic competitiveness. In parts 2 and 3 of this book, I discuss in detail the economic and business effects of these social and demographic changes.

6

Freedom and Human Capital: The New Paradigm

The 1960s brought intense conflict in all elements of U.S. society. The civil rights movement, Vietnam, the women's movement, and economic change all created a period of unusual turbulence. Essentially the 1960s were a second American revolution—a struggle for greater personal freedom in all aspects of life. As the established attitudes of the mature industrial age began to clash with the new attitudes of the knowledge society, a massive shift in attitudes occurred.

The Revolution for Greater Freedom

Although the United States was the center of the revolution for greater freedom, the new paradigm spread around the world in the 1980s. It can be seen in the rise of the Green parties in Western Europe, the spread of democracy in Latin America and Asia, and in the recent upheavals in Eastern Europe. Sometimes it led to violent events like the Tiananmen Square uprising in China. But it also led to the bloodless revolution in Eastern Europe in 1989, which reshaped the face of Europe and drastically altered global politics. Currently it lies at the heart of the efforts to restructure the Soviet Union through perestroika and glasnost.

The revolution is ultimately about the liberation of human

potential and is a direct result of the increasing importance of human capital in the economy and the liberating role of modern computer and communications technology. It is not an accident that college campuses were the center of the upheavals in the United States in the 1960s or that students were the leaders in the demonstrations in China or that intellectuals like playwright Vaclav Havel were the leaders of the peaceful revolution in Eastern Europe. Nor is it an accident that perestroika and glasnost in the Soviet Union were implemented by the best-educated leader in Soviet history. Education in itself is a liberating experience that develops the understanding that freedom is an essential prerequisite to the effective flow of knowledge and the unleashing of creative energies (see box).

You can see the role of technology in this revolution in the experience of China in 1989. The fax machine was the protesting

---

RONALD REAGAN AND THE KNOWLEDGE ECONOMY

In May of 1988 Ronald Reagan visited Moscow for a summit meeting with Soviet President Gorbachev. During that visit President Reagan addressed an audience of students at Moscow State University about the essence of the new knowledge economy and how freedom nourishes it. Below are some excerpts from the speech:

"Like a chrysalis, we are emerging from the economy of the Industrial Revolution, an economy confined and limited by the earth's physical resources, into [one] in which there are no bounds on human imagination and the freedom to create is the most precious natural resource."

"Think of [the] little computer chip. Its value isn't in the sand from which it is made, but in the microscopic architecture designed into it by ingenious human minds."

"In the new economy, human invention increasingly makes physical resources obsolete. We are breaking through the material conditions of existence to a world where man creates his own destiny."

"But progress is not foreordained. The key is freedom—freedom of thought, freedom of information, freedom of communication."

---

students' link to the outside world. One of the first acts taken by the Chinese government in its crackdown was to try to cut off all communication between the students and the outside world. Knowledge and information were the most dangerous threats facing the government. As the Chinese discovered, however, it is impossible to enjoy the full benefits of a modern free market economy without creating pressure for freedom in all areas.

The Emergence of a New Consciousness

The growth of the knowledge society is leading to a new *consciousness,* or new ways of thinking. One author who recognized early the distinctions between the old way of thinking and the new way of thinking was Charles Reich, who wrote the best-selling book *The Greening of America* in 1970. The perspective of time shows that Reich was able to identify the changing world view that subsequently has been incorporated in American society. He distinguished three segments of American history and identified a paradigm, or what he calls *consciousness,* associated with each one—"Consciousness I," "Consciousness II," and "Consciousness III."

Reich defined Consciousness I as the traditional outlook of the American farmer, small businessperson, and worker trying to get ahead. It was essentially the frontier ethic combined with the Puritan ethic of New England and arose as the individual was liberated from the constraints of class status and the settled village life of Europe. The critical goal was to release individual energy held back by rigid social custom and hierarchical forms so that each person could be the source of his or her own achievement and fulfillment. One worked for self, not society. Consciousness I focused on self but in harsh and narrow terms, accepting much self-repression as the essential concomitant of effort and allowing self to be cut off from the larger community of man and from nature (defined as an enemy) as well. The key concepts of Consciousness I were that morality—plainness, character, honesty, hard work, and self-denial—was the key to success; that competition was the law of nature and man; that life was a harsh pursuit of individual self-interest in struggle with fellow men whose nature was fundamentally bad; that life was a "zero sum game"; and that the least government governs best.

Consciousness I was the unique U.S. version of the agricultural society paradigm that existed throughout the old world. The key to the old world agricultural paradigm was a local community orientation. People were born, lived, worked, and died in the same place among people they knew and saw every day. Scale was small, and activity was influenced by nature. Laws were administered by visible local people, and economic activity was rooted in, and subordinated to, the social system. There was no separation between work and living. Community ties were strong and seldom severed. Each person lived within a circle that began before his or her birth, did not depend on personal action, and lasted after death. Food and shelter were communal enterprises; no one grew fat and no one starved alone. Communal traditions in the form of customs or religion were the regulators of life.

Reich's Consciousness II developed as a result of the failure of Consciousness I to deal with the problems of industrialization. As the United States industrialized, it was plagued by robber barons, business piracy, ruinous competition, unreliable products, false advertising, grotesque economic inequality, and the general chaos created by excessive individualism and the lack of coordination and planning. In response, Consciousness II emerged about the time of World War I, took extended root in the period 1930 to 1945 in conjunction with Franklin Roosevelt's New Deal, and emerged fully after World War II. Variations of this paradigm emerged about the same time in the industrial countries of Europe and Japan. Both fascism and Marxism-Leninism are variations of this paradigm.

Consciousness II grew out of the essential principles of industrial society—standardization of products and administrative routines ("scientific management"); specialization and division of labor; professionalism; concentration of energy, population, work, education, and economic organization; and centralization of control and government. The general values flowing from these principles in the mature industrial state were rational use of nation's resources through organization, cooperation, planning, and regulation; maximum utilization of technology and science; meritocracy of equal opportunity and ability; and affirmative government managed by the best educated, most intelligent men operating in the "public interest."

These principles and values were enshrined in the consciousness of the mature industrial state. A hierarchical, elitist, planned, and rational United States developed in which the potential excesses of the private sector were balanced by the public sector's protections of the individual. Realities of the time seemed to demand organization and coordination of activity, the arrangement of things in a rational hierarchy of authority and responsibility, and the dedication of each individual to training, work, and goals beyond himself. The consciousness of the frontier sacrificed for individual good, while the consciousness of the mature industrial society sacrificed for the common good.

Discipline and hierarchy were seen as necessary because society was not yet prepared to offer each person the kind of work he or she wanted or the chance to perform that work with a measure of independence. A central aspect of the consciousness of the mature industrial society was the belief that individual wills and destinies must be linked to institutions, organizations, and society. The "institution man" saw his own life and career in terms of progress within an institution.

The institutional orientation of mature industrial society was examined in detail in William Whyte's bestseller of the 1950s, *The Organization Man.* The organization man accepted established hierarchy and procedures as necessary and valuable. He measured achievement in terms of a meritocracy of education, technical knowledge, and position. Institutions certified the meaning and value of his life and provided personal security in terms of tenure, salary, and retirement benefits. The organization man adopted as his personal values the structure of standards and rewards provided by his occupation or organization and defined individual success and ambitions within these terms. The organization man disclaimed personal responsibility for what his organization did since he was a person without absolute or transcendental values and lacking general authority. He saw life as a fiercely competitive struggle for a success defined by organizational or institutional values and had a strong fear of failure. His own reality was tied to his work. His friends were made through his work (and generally had nothing in common with him after his downfall or departure). He defined happiness in terms of his position in the complex hierarchy of status of his organization.

Reich's Consciousness III started with the self and not with Consciousness II's acceptance of society, the public interest, and institutions as the primary realities. Consciousness III's only commandment was, "Be true to oneself." It postulated the absolute worth of every human being and rejected the whole concept of excellence and comparative merit that was central to Consciousness II. In personal relations, it emphasized honesty, the absence of socially imposed duty, and the rejection of relationships of authority and subservience. Consciousness III had a nonmaterial set of values and embodied the freedom to have nonmaterial goals.

Instead of viewing the world as a jungle where every man competed fiercely for survival (Consciousness I) or as a meritocracy leading to a great corporate hierarchy of rigidly drawn relations and maneuvers for social and economic position (Consciousness II), Consciousness III envisioned a community in which the search for wisdom replaced the competition and separation of the past. In this world, each individual was free to grow toward the highest possibilities of the human spirit. Key values of Consciousness III included respect for each individual's uniqueness and privacy, abstention from coercion or violence against any individual, including war, respect for nature and beauty in all its forms, equality of status between all individuals, and freedom in all aspects of economic and personal life (see box).

A major accomplishment of Consciousness III was to dissolve the link between job and authority and status. Quality, dedication, and excellence were preserved, but work was nonalienated, was the free choice of each person, and was integrated into a full and satisfying life that expressed and affirmed each individual being. A central concept of Consciousness III was the power to change a way of life. When people pursue several careers, either simultaneously or successively, they do not become obsolete due to changing technology.

Events in the 1980s have shown that the underlying philosophy and world view of Consciousness III are increasingly being

---

"WE ARE THE WORLD"

In the mid-1980s Ethiopia suffered from massive famine, and the world saw the sad results of this famine in television pictures of starving babies and small children. The entertainment community in the United States and Britain responded by staging rock concerts in major world cities and developing a rock video to raise funds for famine relief efforts. The video's title song—"We Are the World"—became the theme song of the relief effort and reflected the belief in a single unified world in which everybody is responsible for the children of the world no matter where they live. "We Are the World" was an anthem about an interdependent world whose future will be determined by the quality of experience of the world's children, its future human capital.

In September 1990 this consciousness was further manifested when the leaders of seventy-one member states of the United Nations met at the UN World Summit for Children to sign (along with representatives of over thirty other member states) the Convention on the Rights of the Child. Along with recognizing universal responsibility for the welfare of the world's children, this Convention reflected a growing awareness that reducing poverty requires improving the health and education of the world's children. World leaders are increasingly recognizing that human capital, not showy large industrial projects, is the key to the world's future.

---

incorporated in the outlook of the average American as well as being spread around the world. The key values of Consciousness III are at the heart of the worldwide revolutions for greater freedom. The manifestations of this changing outlook also include the entrepreneurial revolution that is transforming the economy, the civil rights movement, the environmental movement, and the women's movement and women's changing roles, which are transforming both the economy and overall society. Consciousness III represents a response to a world that is being changed dramatically by technology.

The central values of Consciousness III are consistent with a knowledge society in which human capital is the critical economic variable and liberation of human potential the goal of management. Since the paradigm represented by Consciousness III is held more widely among the younger segments of the population, it conflicts with the established values and expectations of Consciousness II. Nevertheless, economic and social trends indicate that Consciousness III is increasingly dominating and shaping U.S. society.

The New Society: Everyone an Individual

Marriage and Parenting Are Choices

The current generation of Americans in their twenties have absorbed the principles of Consciousness III as described by Charles Reich. Various writers have described them as aspiring to be self-sufficient and committing to a lifelong, dynamic relationship with themselves. Paramount among their goals is the desire to know themselves and to express their uniqueness. In fact, an entire generation appears to value qualities common to most entrepreneurs, such as an ability to control one's own destiny and maintain flexibility.

Marriage for both sexes is viewed as desirable but not mandatory, reflecting a fundamental shift in attitude toward voluntary single status. Unlike twenty-five years ago, the majority of young men and almost half the young women between age twenty and twenty-nine are unmarried. At the same time, a new ethos emerging among married couples calls for each partner to be self-sufficient within marriage. A new integrity between the sexes is emerging based on the premise of self-security, fulfillment, and friendship, rendering old rules and roles obsolete. Parenting is viewed as another lifestyle choice and not a necessity. Parents are volunteers in the truest sense, bringing a heightened appreciation for a child's individuality.

Politically, members of this generation are political hybrids who are neoconservatives or neoliberals with traditional liberal positions on minority and women's rights and social liberties but conservative positions on government spending. They could be described as libertarians who are seeking the maximum amount of freedom in both their economic and social lives while tempering individualism with a social and environmental awareness manifested through growing volunteer activities.

Whole-Brain Thinking

The shift to a knowledge society has increasingly emphasized what is called whole-brain thinking. During the industrial age analysis and logic—as outgrowths of society's dependence on mathematics, mechanical engineering, and Newtonian physics— were fostered, and creativity and artistic expression were overlooked. Industrial society became characterized by left-brain thinking—the logical, analytical, mathematical thought that neurosurgeons have determined takes place on the left side of the brain.

In the knowledge economy many routine logical and analytical functions can be best performed by computers, but creative thought is the exclusive ability of human beings. People therefore are increasingly expected to exercise whole-brain thinking by combining logic and analysis with creativity and judgment.

The New World View

Social Values

Comparing descriptions of the generation presently in their twenties with Charles Reich's description of their older brothers and sisters (or parents in some cases) reveals that there has been a fundamental change in the U.S. value system over the last twenty-five years. Current social values are significantly different from the values of those who came of age in the Great Depression and World War II and matured in the advanced industrial society of the 1950s. The key elements of the world view associated with the new knowledge society are summarized and contrasted with that associated with industrial society in table 6.1.

Table 6.1   Basic Social Values in Industrial and Knowledge Societies

Industrial Society	_Knowledge Society_
Hierarchy	Equality
Conformity	Individuality and creativity
Standardization	Diversity
Centralization	Decentralization
Efficiency	Effectiveness
Specialization	Generalist, interdisciplinary, holistic
Maximization of material wealth	Quality of life, conservation of material resources
Emphasis on quantitative content	Emphasis on quality of output
Security	Self-expression and self-actualization

The Political System

This new world view is leading to a new political system through the declining importance of ideology in politics. In an industrializing society ideologies thrive because of the turmoil generated as a rigidly structured rural society is transformed into a dynamic urban one. The newly enfranchised masses are organized by trade unions and political parties and unified by relatively simple ideological programs. In the knowledge society, however, there develops a more pragmatic approach to social problems, along with new concerns with preserving humane values. The individual support of millions of unorganized citizens is effectively marshalled through reliance on television and imagery, which creates a cosmopolitan, although highly impressionistic, involvement in global affairs.

As centers of power shift, the relationship between wealth and social status does as well. The early personalized phase of industrialization economic power tends to evolve toward depersonalized economic power because of the rise of a highly complex interdependence among government, scientific establishments, and industrial organizations. In the knowledge society, large organizations downsize, and entrepreneurship once again personalizes economic power. Similarly, in an industrial society the accumulation of personal wealth is the principal means for social advancement, whereas in the knowledge society social status is derived increasingly from knowledge and personal achievement rather than personal wealth, a change that reflects the principal scarcity in a knowledge society—time, not goods.

When economies shift, the central political and legal issues of the time shift as well. In an industrial society, the political and legal systems grapple with issues emerging from the efficiencies of scale and the centralization of power under industrialization. Issues like protection against unemployment, limitations on and government control of monopolies, the legal right to establish worker unions as a form of worker protection, and the development of a minimum standard of welfare are the central issues of political and legal struggle in an industrial economy. In a knowledge economy, however, the central political and legal issues focus on expansion of individual rights and the removal of impediments to the development and full utilization of human capital. Issues like freedom of expression, removal of government control over private decisions (as in abortion laws), expansion of and equal access to educational opportunities, and removal of barriers to employment and advancement for all members of society are the central issues of political and legal struggle.

THE VICTORY OF AN IDEA: THE HELSINKI SUMMIT OF 1990

The summit meeting of Mikhail Gorbachev and George Bush in Helsinki, Finland, in September 1990 resulted in a remarkable agreement. Instead of being on the opposite side of every world conflict, leaders of the two most militarily powerful countries in the world agreed in front of a worldwide television audience that aggression is counterproductive in an interdependent world and that stopping aggression is a worldwide responsibility.

This joint condemnation of the former Soviet client state of Iraq for aggression against Kuwait and the call for it to withdraw from Kuwait marked a turning point in postwar history. Once cooperation is acknowledged to be more beneficial than competition, the global security and cooperation that are prerequisites to a global knowledge economy can be achieved.

The worldwide shift to knowledge economies that emphasize human capital has resulted in many international political developments. The growing worldwide movement for human rights, the integration of Europe through the European Economic Community (which provides for free movement of labor and common licensing of professionals), and the restructuring of the political systems and economies of Eastern Europe and the Soviet Union away from the centralized control of Communism toward participatory democracy and the free market are all manifestations of the spread of knowledge economies and their related values (see box on previous page).

The shift in values described in this chapter and the dramatic technological and demographic changes occurring in the 1990s are reshaping the environment in which U.S. business operates and the way it must be managed. The next section of the book describes how U.S. business is being changed by these events.

II

THE EFFECT OF THE KNOWLEDGE ECONOMY ON BUSINESS AND MANAGEMENT

7

The Rapid Reshaping of Business Markets and the Labor Force

Changing demographics, social patterns, and production economics due to new technology and new organizational approaches are radically reshaping business markets and the labor force. One trend is for the market for services to grow faster than the market for goods as markets for major consumer goods (such as autos and furniture) become glutted and consumer discretionary income is directed toward services. Another trend is toward greater segmentation of markets as increased individuality and discretionary income generate demand for a broader range of products and services. A third trend is for shifts in demand between individual submarkets within the same basic goods or services sector. Finally, new technology tends to create new markets as it destroys old markets.

Of the various forces reshaping business markets, demographics are probably the most significant. Longer lives and lower birth rates for the post–World War II baby boomers are causing massive shifts in the absolute numbers of consumers in individual market segments and reinforcing the basic market trends (shift from goods to services, splintering into submarkets, and shifting between submarkets). Technological change is the second most significant force reshaping business markets. As new products are developed, they create new markets and destroy old ones. The development of the video cassette recorder has created a market for VCRs as well as a market for videocassette rentals while it has reduced the demand for network television and drive-in movies. Of course, technology indirectly causes demographic change, so it both directly and indirectly reshapes business markets. Demographics also are changing the U.S. labor force by increasing labor shortages as two decades of low birthrates translate into fewer entrants into the workforce and by increasing diversity in the workforce as women and minorities make up a larger percentage of the labor force.

The Shift to Services

In a knowledge economy the demand for services grows at a much faster rate than the demand for goods. Goods tend to be used to satisfy basic physical needs; food, clothing, housing, and automobiles account for most consumer spending on goods. As an affluent population satisfies its basic physical needs, demand for goods plateaus, and demand for services grows. Once you have a full stomach, comfortable clothes, and a warm home, your basic physical needs are met, and you begin to focus on satisfying psychological needs (which services satisfy).

An older population also tends to buy more services than goods, reflecting both an increase in the demand for services like health care and a purchase of many basic goods early in life. As the elderly grow in absolute and relative numbers, they also are growing in relative affluence due to a combination of improved financial support from private and public pension systems, second careers, and strong investment portfolios. Over the past thirty years the number of older persons who live below the poverty line has dropped steadily from 35 percent to less than 12 percent.

Many retirees form a new leisure class, one with money to spend and time to enjoy it. Another equally important characteristic of those age sixty-five and older today is their wish to stay active and be part of the mainstream. Many retirees are returning to part-time or full-time jobs, creating an experienced, capable pool of labor, while another large group is back in school (current estimates are that approximately a million students age sixty-five and older are taking courses). The growth of the population age sixty-five and over and its relative affluence has resulted in the emergence of what advertisers have termed the *maturity market.* Its major characteristic is a growth in demand for services, especially health care services and selected leisure services such as travel services.

Health care expenditures increase dramatically after age forty because of normal physical deterioration associated with age coupled with advances in modern medicine that provide treatments to alleviate many of the medical problems of aging. Former President Reagan provided an example of a healthy, productive older American who nonetheless had significant health care requirements. In the first six years of his presidency President Reagan had medical care covering a colon operation, a prostate operation, skin cancer, and the fitting of two hearing aids. None of these medical treatments was a result of terminal care, and all had the effect of prolonging his life and enhancing his productivity. As the population ages, demands for the type of health care that President Reagan has received will multiply.

Just as the aging of America is creating a mushrooming demand for health care expenditures of all kinds, it is also creating a major expansion of selected leisure markets. In the travel industry many activities like cruises, tours, and resort vacations are marketed to the over-sixty-five market.

With an older average population some markets will stagnate or decline, particularly certain goods markets. The demand for starter housing for young couples and families will decline as they become a smaller segment of the population in both relative and absolute terms. Similarly, the markets for new appliances and new household furnishings will decline. Since the aging of the population has been a result of both longer lives and dropping birthrates, many markets for goods and services that cater to babies, children, and teenagers will shrink.

Shifting markets caused by an aging population are not limited to the United States. Japan has a rapidly aging population, which is creating a huge new market for Japanese business as the number of Japanese over sixty-five increases from 15 million in 1990 to a projected 32 million in 2020. The Asahi Life Insurance Company of Japan has predicted that by the year 2000, the over-sixty-five market in Japan would spend $700 billion annually, creating growth opportunities for a wide range of products and services. Many Japanese businesses are rethinking their marketing strategies as they discover the elderly: an automatic focus camera recently introduced in Japan has proven a hit among the elderly even though it was intended for the youth market.

The Proliferation of Markets

One of the primary characteristics of the knowledge society, along with the shift to services is the proliferation of new markets reflecting the needs of the knowledge society. The forces creating these new markets include affluence, education, and changing lifestyles. The result is a vast array of new market opportunities even as traditional markets for many businesses are shrinking.

When a population lives below or only slightly above the subsistence level, its pattern of needs is comparatively uniform. Food, clothing, shelter, basic medical needs, transportation to and from work, and simple communication needs are universal concerns and therefore can be produced on a standardized basis, taking advantage of long production runs and the classical economies of scale. However, as affluence increases, the range of wants widens, and individual consumers begin to insist that goods or services be tailored to particular tastes (see box).

An economy that provides for a few basic needs is very different than one that supplies the endlessly diverse needs of the ego. Demand for services and customized goods rises as discretionary income is spent on services such as entertainment and education and goods like customized automobiles. These changing demands stimulate the growth of niche markets, such as affluent singles and affluent two-income couples. Singles are large consumers of entertainment, restaurant meals, and expensive gift apparel while affluent two-income couples are major consumers of expensive travel and vacation services.

Affluence increases the range of consumer demands, but so do education, travel, and communications. Knowledge of how other

COMMUNISTS GO TO BUSINESS SCHOOL

By the year 2010 Americans may have stopped worrying about Russian rockets and begun worrying about Russian purchases of U.S. companies. With the advent of perestroika Soviet managers have to learn how to operate in a market economy. This has created a new group of students at American business schools. In 1990 over 200 Soviet managers attended MBA or executive programs at a dozen schools including Harvard and the University of Virginia. This is a 2000 percent increase over the ten Soviet managers who attended programs in 1985.

Marketing is the subject that is hardest for Soviet managers studying at U.S. business schools. In an economy dominated by central planning and lacking competition, the idea that "the customer is king" is a radical departure. Nothing in their experience gives Soviet managers the skills to merchandise in a free market economy. As they learn how to stimulate a market, how to price, how to advertise and promote, they may be the vanguard of a new economic superpower of the twenty-first century.

people live creates demands for a wide range of new goods and services: knowledge of the world increases the demand for foreign food and foreign travel, and, similarly, knowledge of the capability of modern medicine creates a demand for it. Awareness that a thorough physical examination with advanced diagnostic tests can spot cancer and heart problems early will cause people to seek such an exam.

Changes in lifestyles also can cause a proliferation of new markets. Current lifestyle trends that are greatly reshaping business markets include the trend toward more working women, more two-income families (particularly two high-income families), more singles, and more overall affluence. These trends are increasing demands for a wide range of services that compensate for lack of time. Working women have created strong demand for time-saving appliances (microwave ovens, frost-free refrigerators, food processors, and dishwashers) and services that replace many housekeeping functions (fast food restaurants, cleaning services, child care services, and catalogue shopping).

The Consumer Life Cycle

The financial services industry illustrates how changing demographics cause consumers to shift among different submarkets in the same basic market. The financial services business works with a concept known as the consumer financial services life cycle because consumers use different financial services at different points in their lives. A young person has different medical insurance requirements than people in their late fifties. As the post–World War II baby boomers mature and the overall population ages, the size of different age categories in the population will change, resulting in major shifts in demand in the various consumer financial services submarkets. The demand for mortgage services can be expected to level off, while the demand for personal investment services probably will rise dramatically. Regardless of how steady the level of overall consumer spending on financial services, this fluctuating demand will produce major disturbances within the financial services industry.

Technology Creates and Destroys Markets

In a knowledge economy rapidly changing technology generates tremendous turbulence in markets. New markets emerge rapidly as people accept a new technology, but at the same time old markets are destroyed as new technology replaces the old. A good example of such creation and destruction is the business travel industry in the United States. Prior to World War II air travel for business was uncommon; the vast majority of business travel was by train. As aircraft technology improved, however, the airline industry in the United States grew dramatically, so that by 1990 air travel for business is such a standard part of U.S. business that airline strikes or airline failures are front page news because they affect the overall economy.

Today, the computer and communications markets provide similar examples of creation and destruction of markets. From a nonexistent market when the Apple computer was first introduced, the U.S. personal computer market grew over ten years into a $30 billion market (see box). During this dramatic period of growth, companies grew rapidly and prospered and then failed as markets shifted. Osborne Computer introduced the first portable computer and grew rapidly during the early 1980s, but competition from other portable computers that were faster and cheaper resulted in its failure in the mid-1980s.

Another example of how technology creates new markets and destroys old ones is fax communications. As the availability of fax communications grows and its cost drops, it is increasingly replacing overnight and even first-class mail delivery services. During the 1990s fax communications will increasingly replace first-class mail for routine business communications, and as this

---

COMPUTERS: A SALES EXPLOSION

In 1983 there were an estimated 700,000 installed general purpose mainframe computers and minicomputers and 12 million personal computers in the United States, and total U.S. computer sales were $29.8 billion. In the five-year period from 1983 to 1988 overall computer sales in the United States more than doubled from $29.8 billion to $62.6 billion even though computers were declining dramatically in cost. The cause of this sales explosion was growth in sales of microcomputers, popularly known as personal computers or PCs. Between 1981 and 1988 personal computer unit sales steadily increased from 1.1 million in 1981 to 9.5 million in 1988 and from $3.1 billion to $27.7 billion. Total personal computers in use increased from 2.1 million in 1981 to 45.1 million in 1988 or approximately one PC for every five Americans—a good example of how technology can create exploding growth markets.

---

occurs, the postal service will experience with first-class mail the kind of obsolescence that the railroads experienced with passenger service.

From Labor Surpluses to Labor Shortages

As the entry of most American women into the workforce is completed and the low birthrates of the 1960s and 1970s result in lower population growth, qualified new employees will be increasingly difficult to hire. Between 1970 and 1980 the U.S. labor force increased at an annual rate of 2.3 percent. Between 1980 and 1990, however, the annual rate of labor force increase declined to 1.8 percent, and between 1990 and 2000 the U.S. Bureau of Labor Statistics is projecting a further decrease in the labor force growth rate to 1.2 percent annually or approximately half the rate of increase of the 1970s.

Labor shortages as a result of a declining birthrate over the last twenty-five years have been experienced by the advanced economies of Western Europe and Japan as well. In Japan a "baby bust" started about eight years before the U.S. baby bust of the 1960s as a result of the availability of legal abortion in Japan. Japanese unemployment currently stands at 2.1 percent (the lowest rate in the advanced world), and businesses are going bankrupt because of their inability to find staff. Japanese officials say that there are 140 jobs for every job seeker. These shortages are occurring even though Japan has the highest level of automation of the advanced economies and is investing heavily in further automation. It already has one industrial robot for every 700 Japanese (versus the U.S. ratio of one robot for every 7,000 Americans) and expects its new annual investment in robots to grow from $300 million in 1989 to $8.6 billion by 1995. To cope with the labor shortages the Japanese government is encouraging corporations to raise the retirement age from sixty to sixty-five and has opened 425 employment centers for retired workers. In the fall of 1990 the

Japanese government also launched its first job training program for housewives with a pilot effort in Tokyo and plans to extend nationwide.

In the European Economic Community, the current fertility rate is 1.58 (well below the replacement rate of 2.1 per woman). Despite current European social backlash against immigration demographers are predicting that Europe will have to extensively import labor from areas like North Africa early in the twenty-first century in order to prevent a decline in its economy. Substantial increased immigration in the future as a result of labor shortages promises to be a major social problem.

Diversity: The Hallmark of the New Workforce

In 1985, 47 percent of the workforce in the United States was native-born white males, but they are expected to account for only 15 percent of the 25 million projected new entries to the workforce between 1985 and 2000. An influx of white women, nonwhites, and immigrants into the U.S. workforce will dramatically increase its diversity, particularly among younger workers. In the future, you will increasingly find that the best man for the job may be a Hispanic woman.

Because immigration is predominantly from non-European and Third World countries, the United States is experiencing substantial changes in its overall racial and ethnic mix. As the United States becomes a more racially heterogeneous society, whites make up a smaller portion of the total population and other racial groups individually grow more rapidly in size. The United States is shifting from a society in which whites and blacks were its principal racial groups to a society in which whites, blacks, Hispanics, and Asians will all be major groups (see box).

The rapid growth in number of Asians has a particular significance for the knowledge economy, since they tend to demonstrate the traditional immigrant characteristics of hard work and

---

IMMIGRATION AND AMERICA'S CHANGING FACE

In the fall of 1990 a new museum of immigration was dedicated on Ellis Island, which from 1892 to 1954 was the first stop for immigrants to the United States arriving in the port of New York. Almost 100 million Americans, 40 percent of the U.S. population, trace their roots to a relative who passed through Ellis Island. America is a land of immigrants.

In the decade of 1980 to 1990 the United States received immigrants in record numbers, setting a new record for the most immigrants received in a single decade. In the 1980s over 10 million immigrants entered the United States, surpassing the old record of 8.8 million who arrived between 1900 and 1910. The United States is receiving immigrants in record numbers, but they are coming from different parts of the world than previous immigrants: in 1910, 89 percent of immigrants to the United States were Europeans; in 1990, 10 percent were Europeans.

Most of the new immigrants to the United States since the decade of the 1960s have been from Asia and Latin America. The result has been a reshaping of the country into a true microcosm of the world community. All races and most nationalities are becoming well represented in the mosaic of its population.

---

achievement. Of Asian adults, over one-third have finished college versus approximately one-fifth of the white population.

The Managerial Implications of Changing Markets and the Changing Labor Force

The managerial implications of the changes in markets and the labor force are enormous. From demographic shifts alone, there will be major market turbulence in the future. Changing buying patterns will result from the changing needs of age, greater affluence, and new and diverse lifestyles. When the impact of new unknown social patterns and new unknown technology are added to the clear demographic shifts, the probability is overwhelming of continued rapid change in markets. Examples of questions managers will have to ask include: How will social patterns change when half of the females in the U.S. over 40 are single (as current projections of divorce and remarriage would indicate for women of the baby boom generation)? How will markets be affected by the availability of a low-cost, effective home picturephone?

In terms of their workforce, managers will no longer be able to expect that the majority will be made up of white men who are motivated by being the primary breadwinner for a family with a wife at home to take care of the family's domestic needs. They increasingly will be forced to deal with social and cultural problems such as child care and elder care issues, language barriers, and legal issues relating to immigration. Management style will increasingly have to take account of differences between different cultures and different sexes. In areas like promotion, managers will be forced to be gender blind and color blind by the simple availability of qualified candidates rather than the legal pressure of affirmative action.

Changes in the labor force and shortages of skilled workers will pressure managers to improve the quality of the labor force and use employees more effectively through training and attractive personnel policies. Companies also will be pressured to increase their capital investment per worker and automate routine jobs wherever possible. In chapter 10 I discuss the changing management philosophies that are evolving with the need for a better trained workforce. The next chapter examines how automation is increasingly affecting almost every sector of the economy.

8

The Changing Economics
of Operations

The production or operations side of business is being drastically affected by new computer, communications, and robotics technology. In agriculture, manufacturing, and services, computers, robotics, and related technology are dramatically affecting production economics and productivity. Robots increasingly displace assembly line workers, while computers displace middle managers (see chapter 4). Computers and automation are affecting every type of business and promise a productivity explosion in the 1990s.

It is now known that the automation of manufacturing will raise productivity and shift workers to the service sector, but computers are affecting every service sector as well—improving productivity, improving the quality of services, changing the economics of operations, and creating tremendous managerial strains. As labor shifts toward knowledge services from the other service sectors, the productivity and quality of the full spectrum of knowledge services will improve.

Capital Investment and Productivity

It is a principle of economics that the more capital investment per worker, the greater the productivity of the worker. Capital investment made in the form of education and training allows the educated and trained worker to be more effective in using physical capital—computer, communications, and robotics technologies—and in performing various aspects of his or her work. These investments can be successful across a wide range of industries if the necessary investment in training is made.

The opportunities for productivity improvements in the manufacturing sector have been discussed in earlier chapters, but the long-term potential for productivity improvement in the service sector equals or exceeds that of manufacturing because information businesses can be drastically reshaped by emerging computer technology. Looking at relative capital investment, the lower the investment per worker in an area, the greater the potential relative payoff of an investment in automation and labor reduction. Figure 8.1 summarizes relative capital investment per worker in different goods-producing and service operations. As the figure shows, goods-producing activities have been much more capital intensive than service industries, particularly knowledge service industries like health care and education. This situation is changing with the growth and expansion of computer technology. Computer technology and automation allow service businesses to reduce costs and to improve both the quality and range of their products, providing more and better services. In the future, the rate of application of computer technology to services should accelerate.

The Automation of Manufacturing

Robotics and related technology bring about major changes in manufacturing that result in higher productivity and lower employment. Of the 25,000 industrial robots installed in factories around the world in 1982, the U.S. accounted for approximately 6,000 and Japan for approximately 13,000. By the year 1990 U.S. industry had over 25,000 robots in place and Japan had over 150,000. By the year 1995 the Robotics Industry Association predicts that nearly a quarter of a million robots will be operating in the United States.

By the year 2000 it is estimated that 50 to 75 percent of all U.S.

Figure 8.1   Capital Invested per Person in Specific Industries, 1985

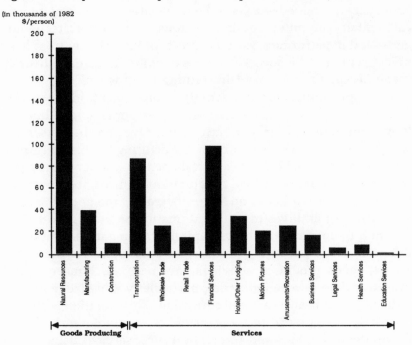

(in thousands of 1982 $/person)

Source: Computed from data in *Technology and the American Economic Transition* (Washington, D.C.: Office of Technology Assessment, U.S. Congress, 1988).

factory production jobs—up to 1 million workers a year for the rest of the century—will be replaced by industrial robots. Looking further into the future, Peter Drucker estimates that by 2010 only 5 percent of the U.S. workforce will be involved in manufacturing versus almost 20 percent today (see box).

This growth in the use of robots is being spurred by economics. Thirty robot welders can replace forty to fifty human welders and at the same time increase overall productivity per hour from sixty cars for a human welder to one hundred cars for the robot welder. Since the cost of an industrial robot is often equivalent to the one-year cost for an industrial worker's salary and benefits, the greater productivity of the industrial robot makes it a more cost-efficient replacement for the human worker. This is particularly true when the problems of illness, strikes, and other disruptions

---

FACTORY OF THE FUTURE: A PLANT WITH NO WORKERS

The factory of the future is already here. In Charlottesville, Virginia, a college town located in the foothills of the Blue Ridge Mountains of Virginia, GE-Fanuc has located a very unusual factory. GE-Fanuc, a joint venture of General Electric and Fanuc, a Japanese firm that is the world's leading manufacturer of robots, makes control devices for automated machine tools. What is unusual about this plant is that it has no production workers: the basic manufacturing process is totally automated (though humans are used to supervise the machines). Automated equipment such as a Fanuc robot retrieves parts from an automated assembly line, performs the necessary operation, and returns the parts to the line.

Fanuc's plants in Japan show the ultimate future of manufacturing—robots making robots. No workers, not even supervisors, appear on the factory floor. All operations, from material handling to machine operations, are automated. Fanuc's approach to manufacturing is a success. In fact, Fanuc may be the most profitable manufacturing company in the world—with sales per employee of over $1 million, manufacturing margins of more than 45 percent, and pretax margins in excess of 30 percent.

---

of the workplace are added to the cost of the human worker. GM estimated in the early 1980s that 14,000 robots could replace between 40,000 and 50,000 workers (a number equivalent to Chrysler's total hourly workforce) and that 50 percent of GE factory floor workers could be replaced cost effectively with existing automation technology.

Automation of Basic Services: Utilities and Transportation

The utility sector, particularly telecommunications, is a major user of computers and automation. Much early computer technology including the semiconductor was invented at AT&T's Bell Labs, and the telephone system of the United States is essentially the world's largest computer network. In the future the telecom-

munications industry can expect to be a leader in computeriza-
tion/automation of its operations. At the same time, information-related businesses, such as integrated computer-based information systems, depend on the communication and electronics
industry to provide their service to the customer.

Computers, advanced communication, and robotics technology
are used throughout the transportation sector. Air transportation
uses fixed-sequence robots (baggage conveyors), variable-se-
quence robots (automatic air ticketing machines), intelligent robots (autopilot), and totally automated systems (a Boeing 747
making an instrument landing in a snow storm). Similarly, pipeline technology employs highly sophisticated instrumentation,
pumps, and computer-controlled systems. The pipeline itself can
be viewed as a fixed-sequence robot, and a modern pipeline network and management system approaches a totally automated
system. Railroad car tracking systems are computerized as are
electronic navigation systems for ships.

Automation of the Distribution and Hospitality Sectors

The distribution and hospitality sectors of the economy—including wholesale and retail trade, hotels, and restaurants—are
among the largest and most labor-intensive service activities. As
labor costs rise, these sectors will increasingly use computers and
automation to reduce costs and improve productivity, resulting in
massive consolidation of these activities and stagnating or declining employment in these sectors.

Computerization and automation already have affected the operations of wholesale and retail trade. Examples of current automation include automated warehousing, computer-aided auto re-
pair, dry cleaning conveyors, optical bar-scanning equipment,
point-of-sale terminals, electronic shopping, electronic theft and
burglar systems, and automated car washes as well as the use of
computers in the office for payroll, pricing, billing, and inventory
control. In the future, many of the steps in traditional retailing
may be bypassed as more automated systems come into use.

Historically, manufacturers sold to wholesalers, who resold goods to retailers, who sold to final buyers. Goods were typically handled, invoiced, counted, stocked, marked up, insured, and financed many times before they were put into use. In the future, rapidly growing direct catalog sales will bypass the entire wholesale/retail distribution system. Video cassettes of available products, computerized inventory management, and effective overnight delivery will dramatically increase the effectiveness of this approach (see box).

Technology also may lead to great productivity gains at the shopping mall. In the future, the self-service store may become fully automated except for stocking clerks. A store may have an automated checkout system in which the consumer inserts a bank card and then places items to be purchased on a conveyor belt leading to an automatic laser bar-code reader. At the end of the belt a specially adapted pick-and-place robot would bag the items and hand the consumer a receipt.

THE FUTURE IS VIDEO

Laser-disc players coupled with computers soon will revolutionize communication with the retail consumer. Laser-disc players permit the storage of large amounts of visual or video information coupled with the ability to access that information on a random basis, something not possible with the tape medium used in videocassettes. Customers will be able to instantly access a wide variety of prerecorded video information about a corporation's products and services.

Many major companies, including Sears, General Motors, and American Express, have experimented with laser-disc technology as a way to communicate more effectively with their customers. American Express has experimented with combining laser disc technology and computers to develop a fully automated travel office: customers will use the laser-disc player to look at films and slides on vacation spots and review available hotel accommodations, use a computerized reservation system to make reservations and receive tickets, and use a credit card and card reader to make payment.

At first glance, hotel/motel service seems to offer few or no opportunities for automation. The operations function of the hotel/motel, however, depends on computers and automation in a variety of ways, including electronic reservation systems, electronic messages and wake-up systems, electronic key and lock systems, automatic washers and ironing machines, automated cleanup vacuum, and wash and wax machines called "Billygoats." Automation of hotel/motel service improves the quality and timeliness of service, minimizes the operating cost of the hotel/motel, increases capacity (guest room, exhibit hall, dining hall) usage of the hotel/motel, and reduces the number of employees needed to provide the service. In the restaurant and food service business the fixed-sequence vending machine is the simplest form of automation for food services. Vending machines replace people as a means to provide convenient, low-cost food to high- or low-demand locations. A highly sophisticated and computer-controlled vending machine may become the fast food restaurant of the future.

Automation of Financial Services

After telecommunications, financial services is probably the industry most affected by computers and automation. Financial services were some of the earliest users of traditional mainframe computers and have been among the biggest users of computers and automation. Money in a sense is information in motion, and the financial services industry basically deals in the movement and manipulation of that information. The electronic revolution has totally changed the way that this information is moved.

Historically, internal financial industry operations—processing checks or processing securities or communicating about investments—required massive paper flows. Financial transactions no longer require a paper trail and paper documents: they are becoming little blips in the computer. The classic example of this occurred in 1987 when the U.S. Treasury Department stopped issuing certificates for treasury securities. Instead, ownership of securities will be noted in a computer bank, and no actual T-bill or government bond will ever be issued.

The pace of computerization and automation of all aspects of financial services companies can be expected to accelerate in the future. New generations of computer technology will increasingly lower the cost of automating financial services activities, while new artificial intelligence software will expand the types of activities that can be automated, reducing the need for both clerical and middle-management personnel.

In between the financial institution and its customer, computer links are replacing the traditional person-to-person method of conducting business. The most significant example of this is the automatic teller machine. From an expensive customer convenience in the mid-1970s, ATMs became the core of consumer banking systems around the country by the mid-1980s as ATM networks reached transaction levels where total costs per transaction fell below the cost of performing these transactions at the teller window. From a handful of ATMs in the early 1970s the number grew to 28,000 by 1982 compared to 40,000 branch offices at that time. By the year 2000 it is estimated that branch offices may drop to less than 5,000 and electronic access to the banking system will involve 500,000 formal access points—including ATMs, point-of-sale terminals, and other electronic devices. Future relationships between the financial institution and its customer will be even more completely automated. Home banking through the use of microcomputers and the consumer's television set will become routine as will point-of-sale terminals that allow customers to use debit cards to directly charge their accounts for purchases made from retail establishments. By the year 2000, financial services will become one of the most highly automated industries.

Automation of Knowledge Services

Today, over 50 percent of the total U.S. workforce is engaged in knowledge- or information-related services, including financial services, telephone services, postal service, insurance services, newspaper and television services, travel agencies, education services, leisure activities, real estate services, and government services. The growing use of computer technology to improve both the productivity of knowledge services and their quality will dramatically affect the U.S. economy in the last decade of the century.

Long-term projections show that by the year 2000 every office desk will be equipped with either a personal computer or a terminal for access to one. That projection is already a reality for the majority of U.S. businesses because of the dropping cost of computer equipment and the potential productivity increases that it offers to office workers. The average word processing machine, for example, sharply increases secretarial productivity and has dropped from a price of $25,000 per unit when it was originally introduced in the late 1970s to a current price of less than $1,000 per unit.

Further fueling this growth is the low level of capital investment in today's office. Currently the average investment per office worker is approximately one-tenth the average investment per factory worker. With the low level of current capital investment and the increasingly lower costs for office equipment, the potential return on investment in new forms of office equipment that dramatically improve productivity is very high.

Widely varying knowledge and information services are benefitting from the dropping cost and improving capabilities of computer technology and office automation. Many routine legal activities like doing research, drafting documents and pleadings, and providing standard advice can be partially or fully automated. Already law students use personal computers routinely for drafting documents, and computer database research tools like Lexis are a standard tool of the modern law firm. The use of computers and automation in the legal profession should grow rapidly as competitive pressures lead to efforts to cut costs and improve productivity.

Health care is a major user of high-technology equipment of all kinds, including computers and related automation. Automation in health services takes many forms with basically six types of medical technologies—the four hard technologies, which are diagnostic (CAT scanner, automated clinical labs, fetal monitor, computerized electrocardiography), survival (cardiopulmonary bypass machines, iron lung), illness management (pacemaker, renal dialysis machines), and system management (hospital and medical information systems, telemedicine), and the soft technologies, which are the cure or prevention technologies (organ transplant, diet, vaccine). The hard technologies require major expenditures in capital equipment (see box).

The productivity of education systems has remained fundamentally unchanged since the days of Socrates. It historically has been an extremely labor-intensive service industry. Teachers still stand in front of classes and deliver lectures to assembled groups of students. Learning per class hour or per teacher hour has shown little change in response to variations in the organization of school systems, teacher salaries, textbooks, or audiovisual aids. Today's technology, if fully applied, could revolutionize education as dramatically as the automatic loom changed the textile industry (see box). Sophisticated microcomputers are changing the labor-to-capital-equipment ratio in the classroom. Hand-held and desk-top computers are becoming as basic to some classrooms as chalk and the blackboard. When Texas Instruments introduced Speak and Spell in 1978, electronic learning began for the general public. Education services represent a new multibillion-dollar market for electronic learning aids. Automation in the classroom and at home through personal computers allows children to learn at their own pace and frees the teacher from time-consuming and repetitive tasks to focus on individual child development.

The leisure sector is being substantially affected by computeri-

---

TECHNOLOGY AND HEALTH CARE COSTS

A major cause of rising health care costs is the increasing use of high technology, which is used primarily to improve the quality of care rather than to reduce costs. At Massachusetts General Hospital (a teaching hospital of the Harvard Medical School) many new skills were needed when advanced equipment in areas like nuclear medicine was introduced in the 1960s and 1970s. The hospital hired medical systems analysts, computer programmers, biomedical engineers, specially trained nurses and medical technicians (to draw and analyze blood for complex new tests, such as radioimmunossays), radiation therapists, and physicists. In the knowledge economy, new technology works both ways: it can increase or decrease jobs and costs depending on its purpose.

THE CLASSROOM OF THE FUTURE

The classroom of the late 1990s could be a set of individual computer screens linked to massive information storage systems controlled by sophisticated software. The student would have instant electronic access to the best teachers, the most stimulating lessons, and the world's libraries of books, music, or film, assisted by teachers who are guides to the technology and the information sources rather than custodians of the knowledge. With individualized courses, self-paced instruction, and built-in testing, scoring, and evaluation of progress, the modern classroom could provide the equivalent of a personal tutor for each student. The part of education that involves progressive mastery of large bodies of information could be handled with far fewer lectures, freeing teachers for the more challenging tasks of designing and developing courses, leading group discussion, or probing the limits of knowledge.

---

zation and automation. A visit to Walt Disney World and EPCOT—to the Hall of Presidents, the Jungle Cruise, Country Bear Jamboree, the Haunted Mansion, Circle-Vision 360, and Mission to Mars—is a preview of how automation can be used to entertain people. Atari video games, video-yearbooks, and the Betamax portable videocassette recorder are other examples of automated leisure services. As in medicine, computer technology in entertainment has been used primarily to improve the quality of the service and only secondarily to improve its efficiency. In the future, increasing use of automation and computer simulation will provide whole new forms of entertainment. One can imagine neighborhood entertainment centers where advanced video and computer technology allows individuals to travel to all parts of the world or experience a range of adventures such as flying a jet or deep sea diving.

Automation of Government

Historically, government services were considered incapable of productivity increases, but because they are primarily information services of one form or another they can be made more efficient by computerization and automation. Automation in the public and government services takes many forms, including the computerized records of the Social Security Administration, totally automated systems used to operate fossil and nuclear power generating plants, and computerized auditing of tax returns. The extent to which government services incorporate new computer and communication technology such as electronic switchboards, word processors, high-speed printers, teleconferencing, electronic mail, and voice-actuated devices will depend on how strong political pressures are to maintain and expand services while cutting costs since traditional profit motives don't apply in this sector.

For example, in 1982 the federal government employed 171,000 secretaries, stenographers, and typists, or 11.5 percent of all civilian workers in this category. During this time, Atlantic Richfield Co. of Los Angeles cut its ratio of secretaries to administrative personnel from one to five to one to nineteen by installing an integrated central word processing system. A reduction in government secretarial levels similar to that of Atlantic Richfield would have put 126,000 federal employees out of work.

The changing economics of operations coupled with changing markets (which were discussed in the preceding chapter) will require radically new organizational and managerial approaches. These new organizational and managerial approaches are discussed in the next two chapters.

9

The Business Organization Redefined

The shift from an industrial to a knowledge economy is affecting all facets of business—markets, operations, structure, and management theory and techniques. Changing markets and operations require a radically different business organization—one that facilitates the free flow of information, encourages the full use of the brainpower of all its workers, and ensures rapid response to change.

Managerial Belief Systems and Organizational Structure

Most managers want to pursue business-as-usual, a dangerous attitude to hold in an environment that is continually changing. As the economy shifts from industrial to knowledge, many traditional managers find that the successful habits of a lifetime become more counterproductive. The same is true for organizations. The very products, procedures, and organizational forms that helped businesses succeed in the past often prove their undoing. The first rule of survival is clear: the adaptive manager today must be capable of radical action—to reconceptualize products, procedures, programs, and purposes before crisis makes drastic change inescapable. Today organizational change must assume that:

- The structure of a company must be appropriate to its total external environment and not just one dimension of its environment.
- The corporate environment has changed so swiftly and fundamentally in the past two decades that structures designed for success in an industrial environment are almost by definition inappropriate.
- Many key beliefs about organizations must be reexamined. If basic notions about standardization, economies of scale, vertical integration, employee motivation, mass production and distribution, consumer preferences, and hierarchy are no longer valid, policies based on them will drive the organization in the wrong direction.
- In a period of rapid change, planning needs not a set of isolated trends but multidimensional models that interrelate technological, social, political, and cultural forces with economic forces.

At one end of the management continuum managers assume continuity, adopt straight-line strategies, and define problems in isolation from other issues. At the other end of the continuum managers recognize the growing importance of discontinuity, think in nonlinear terms, and define problems in relationship to one another. One kind of manager is good at "thinkable" solutions to problems—a leadership style that is adequate in periods of environmental stability. The other is open to "unthinkable" solutions—a style that may be necessary in periods of environmental turbulence.

Every business has a belief system—and it is at least as important as its accounting system or its authority system. When a society is hit by a wave of technological change, it is forced to reexamine its beliefs. In the same way, a company may find its belief system inappropriate to the new economic and social conditions. Identifying obsolete corporate assumptions is difficult, however, because the most important beliefs are the ones that are least often discussed. The new environment of the knowledge economy requires a new style of corporation and a new business belief system.

The Changing Environment for Organizations

Under industrialization bureaucracy was the dominant form of organization. The factory was intended to produce standardized products; the bureaucracy, to produce standardized decisions. Most major corporations developed in an industrial society, based on a bureaucratic model of machine-like division of function, routine activity, permanence, and a very long vertical hierarchy. It was a world of mass markets, uniform goods and services, and long production runs.

Since the mid-1950s, however, U.S. business has confronted an increasing diversity of lifestyle, opinion, dress, family structure, and consumer need coupled with radical changes in major technology. These changes have radically reshaped the external and internal environment of major corporations. Technology is probably the biggest single factor in destandardization. The technology of the industrial age standardized not only output but work and the people who performed it. While industrial machines standardized, however, computers and robotics destandardize.

The most significant effect of this technology has been the shift from very long to relatively short production runs, in manufacturing and nonmanufacturing operations as well. This step-by-step development from handcraft to mass production to a new, higher form of handcraft is a critical component of the knowledge economy. In the past the company that knew how to standardize most effectively was able to outperform its competitors; in the future the company that knows how to destandardize effectively will be the victor.

Innovation is another important but little understood aspect of organizational success. If R&D results in a flow of new product, how does that innovation affect diversification of product line and organizational structure? Innovation goes beyond just products or even technologies, however, and involves people. At times a firm must cope with very high levels of novelty, and at other times the novelty level is low. Low novelty requires incremental management; high novelty may need radical management. The push toward destandardization forces a company to engage in what might be called additive innovation: that is, to keep up with the demands of a fast-fragmenting marketplace, a company adds model, size, style, and service variation to its line. Simultaneously, however, the rapid pace of technological change compels the same company to engage increasingly in substitutive innovation—the creation of new products, technologies, processes, or procedures to take the place of, or eliminate, old ones.

In a period of intense, accelerated change all management assumptions about the world have to be rechecked for accuracy. Although the industrial society that gave birth to most major corporations was characterized by relatively high consensus and shared values, the knowledge economy has value diversity. Moreover, the technological advances in communications that now make it possible for each group to have its own channels of communications, both electronic and print, encourage social diversity and greater individuality, which then translates into a demand for even more varied services.

From Pyramid to Living Organism

Business organizations are being restructured to eliminate layers of hierarchy suited for managing large numbers of workers in unskilled physical production and to create new structures that facilitate flexibility in communications among highly educated and skilled knowledge workers (see box). Similarly, corporations are being formed and dissolved at a rapid rate as they are viewed increasingly as business conveniences rather than permanent institutions.

Replacing the traditional hierarchical or pyramidal organization of the industrial age is a new form of company—the entrepreneurial knowledge services company—operating in such fields

---

CELLULAR TELEPHONES: TAKING BUSINESS ON THE ROAD

The cellular telephone industry expects to have 100 million cellular phones in use worldwide by the year 2000. By then Motorola expects to have in use a satellite system that will allow users to call from anywhere in the world including the middle of the Amazon or Antarctica. As fax technology is coupled with cellular technology, business units will be able to locate in areas of lowest costs, fewest environmental problems, or nearest markets. As communications present fewer obstacles to doing business, geography will have less influence on business decisions. More businesses will organize functionally on a global basis.

---

as computer software, specialty manufacturing, law, consulting, specialty retailing, and medical services. These companies generally will be small to facilitate the development of proprietary knowledge and the flexibility necessary for innovation.

The management of an entrepreneurial firm perceives opportunities for innovation and provides the marketplace with those innovations. McDonald's in its growth phase is an example of such a company: it perceived the opportunity to streamline and standardize fast-food preparation. A knowledge company's primary resource and principal competitive advantage is the knowledge that its employees possess, which may or may not be captured in some form of intellectual property such as patented drugs, copyrighted books, or proprietary software. Lotus is an example of such a company.

The emerging economy will be based on four basic types of companies—(1) capital-intensive, highly automated companies found primarily in the manufacturing, utility, and natural resource industries; (2) labor-intensive manufacturing with protected market niches, such as food processing companies; (3) non-knowledge-intensive or routine service businesses that use a high degree of automation; and (4) knowledge-intensive service businesses, which will become increasingly dominant organizations in the economy. These organizations will be found in a variety of sectors including financial services, health care services, professional services (consulting, accounting, law, engineering, and architecture), educational software services, computer software firms, scientific research firms, and entertainment.

The Collapsible Corporation

In the knowledge economy, bureaucracy will increasingly be replaced by *adhocracy,* a holding company that coordinates the work of numerous temporary work units, each phasing in and out of existence according to the rate of change in the environment surrounding the organization. The adhocracies of tomorrow will be staffed by employees who are capable of rapid learning (in order to comprehend novel circumstances and problems) and imaginative thinking (in order to invent new solutions). These men and women will participate in small teams, cross-disciplinary teams, partnerships, and quality circles.

The Individual as Business Organization

In the new economy, many individuals become independent contractors, increasingly self-employed and plugging into various organizations during different phases of their careers. The most successful corporations will foster personal growth to attract the best and brightest people. To reinforce synergy between the individual and organization, employers will offer flexible hours, intellectually stimulating environments, lateral moves, multidimensional jobs, and experienced senior people working with younger people. Benefits will be tied less to time and place and more to productivity and contribution and will reflect the various lifestyles of individual employees. Financial and psychic equity in the company will become increasingly important parts of the overall compensation package.

The Changing Role of Capital

In the knowledge economy, the primary function of financial and physical capital will be to release the potential and upgrade the productivity of knowledge workers and not to be the primary means of production. In the industrial age work was organized around physical capital. Work, in terms of shifts and the nature of jobs, was specifically designed to maximize the output of the steel mill; the physical equipment was primary, and the human workers were secondary. Similarly, in the traditional automobile assembly plant work tasks were geared to the rhythm and speed of the assembly line. In fact, a common technique for attempting to improve the productivity of the workforce was to speed up the assembly line.

In contrast, the computer enhances the productivity of the human being. Office workers who are analyzing problems are not tied to the pace of the personal computer on their desks. Rather, the computer responds to the human worker, even to the point of holding data on its screen for many minutes or even hours while the human worker is engaged in another task. As the cost of computer technology comes down, capital investment relating to computers will be secondary to maximizing the output of skilled knowledge workers whose wages comprise the primary cost of the organization.

An Organizational Comparison: U.S. Steel and Merck

The differences between an industrial physical capital–based company and a postindustrial knowledge/human capital–based organization can be seen by examining some key characteristics of U.S. Steel (the premier company of the basic industrial period in the United States) and Merck (one of the premier companies of the knowledge economy) (see table 9.1). Historically, U.S. Steel, like the most classic industrial companies, was organized on the command and control model with a hierarchical structure that was patterned after the military model. The sharp division between management and labor was comparable to that between officers and enlisted men in the military. Decisions went up and down the formal chain of command in both the military and U.S. Steel between the different levels of authority—generals or top management, junior and middle-level officers or middle manage-

Table 9.1 Comparison of United States Steel and Merck

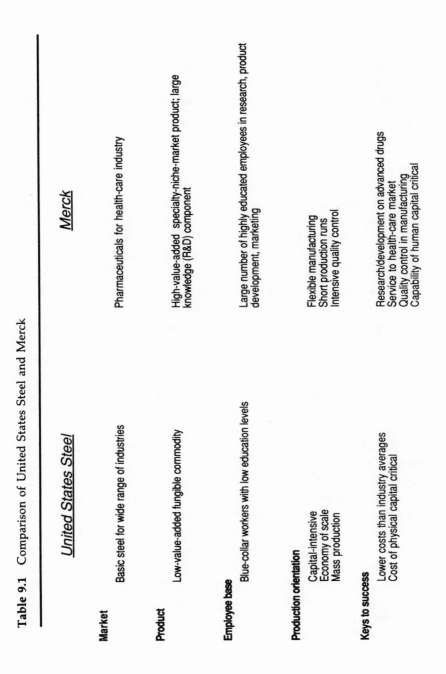

	United States Steel	**Merck**
Market	Basic steel for wide range of industries	Pharmaceuticals for health-care industry
Product	Low-value-added fungible commodity	High-value-added specialty-niche-market product; large knowledge (R&D) component
Employee base	Blue-collar workers with low education levels	Large number of highly educated employees in research, product development, marketing
Production orientation	Capital-intensive Economy of scale Mass production	Flexible manufacturing Short production runs Intensive quality control
Keys to success	Lower costs than industry averages Cost of physical capital critical	Research/development on advanced drugs Service to health-care market Quality control in manufacturing Capability of human capital critical

ment, noncommissioned officers or foremen, soldiers or workers. Giving orders and following orders was the standard pattern of communication and response in both organizations, and little effort was made to tap the knowledge or enlist the brainpower of lower-level members.

Merck, by contrast, represents the emerging information-based organization of the future. A knowledge-based or information-based organization is composed largely of well-educated specialists who direct and discipline their own performance through organized feedback from colleagues, customers, and headquarters. This organization is characterized by few management levels, small central management staffs, and decentralization. Informal teams play a central role in carrying out the critical tasks of the organization as knowledge specialists are deployed and redeployed to use their expertise on the task at hand.

Merck's key resource is its research staff, a large group of scientists ranging from microbiologists to biochemists supported by a budget of over a half billion dollars. These specialists are not organized in a formal hierarchy of the traditional industrial model but instead according to twelve research disciplines and informal cross-discipline project teams. Each project is headed by a leader who must recruit team members from different disciplines to commit their own resources to the project based on its promise. In short, the project leader serves as an entrepreneur, and the research discipline as a venture capitalist.

From a lackluster performance with few new products in 1975 (when the research department structure was revamped under Ray Vangelas, Merck's current chairman), Merck has created a steady stream of new products, has become the most admired large company in the United States (according to a *Fortune* article of 1986), is the darling of Wall Street (contrast its 400 percent increase in market value between 1985 and 1987, a market value five times its annual revenues, with General Motors' market value equal to 25 percent of its annual revenues), and is ranked among the ten largest U.S. companies in market value. During the same period U.S. Steel, the classic traditional industrial company, was in terrible financial shape, and its market value was a fraction of Merck's despite similar revenues.

The Managerial Implications of the New Business Organization

Employees of these new business organizations can no longer expect highly structured lines of authority or clearly defined career ladders. Managers can no longer expect to motivate employees through fear or unreciprocated feelings of corporate loyalty. Employees will increasingly view jobs in terms of their own professional development and will expect employers to provide training and professional opportunities. In the tightening labor market of the 1990s this will require new management styles—the subject of chapter 10.

10

The Revolution in
Management Theory

Twenty years ago most colleges and graduate schools taught
management theory as it applied to the large industrial organizations that were the cornerstone of the mature industrial economy.
Unfortunately, this theory is of little value in the daily work of
today's executives. Frederick Taylor's time and motion studies of
factory workers have limited applicability in a knowledge economy characterized by service companies, large concentrations of
knowledge workers, the computer, and rapid change. The new
approaches of management experts like Peter Drucker are required.

The Difference between Manufacturing
and Services

Service companies dominate the new economy, and even manufacturing companies are becoming more service oriented. They
differ from each other in the following key ways:

- Manufacturing produces a physical, tangible good; a service
  is a package of explicit and implicit benefits performed with
  a supporting facility and using facilitating goods.

- The production of a manufactured good and most of its delivery is accomplished before the customer enters the picture; customers usually participate actively in the production and service delivery system (in self-service supermarkets, for example).
- Generally, the demand for services is time dependent, and failure to deliver the service at the appropriate time results in total loss of value for that unit of service (an empty airline seat or an unbilled hour of a lawyer's time can't be sold at some future time unlike a manufactured good).
- In manufacturing, peaks and valleys in demand can be managed by inventory buffers. Because services are time dependent, their output is noninventoriable. A level provision of a service over time results in unmet demand at peak periods and unused capacity in slack times, making capacity management crucial to the success of a service firm.
- Manufacturing companies benefit from economies of scale; service organizations normally are small and near the customer, resulting in a decentralized structure with many small units of capacity (restaurants, post offices, schools, libraries, hospitals, and banks need to be convenient to the customer).
- Manufacturing companies can establish a competitive advantage through a patented product or technology; it is hard for a service firm to protect a unique service from duplication (although there is some legal protection offered through copyrights, trademarks, and professional licensing).
- Manufacturing is prone to boom and bust cycles when inventory is not meeting customer demand; because of their noninventoriable output service firms' cycles are more moderate.
- Goods are generally more vulnerable to foreign competition because of services' special characteristics. A retail store in England, for example, is of no use to a consumer in New York. Because of other characteristics, however, such as the need for geographic proximity to the customer, and time dependent demand, not all services are immune to foreign

competition. For example, financial services in the United States are increasingly being subject to foreign competition.

- Unlike with manufacturing workers, the interpersonal skills of service workers are critical to the quality of professional services like law, medicine, and architecture and also many mundane services in which workers deal directly with customers. A clean, cheerful, polite, and fast service worker at the counter of a fast-food restaurant is essential to business success.

Management Strategies for Services

Successful management of services requires more than successful financial and asset management. Some strategies include:

- Automation, to provide service capacity where and when the customer wants it (ATMs are examples of this use of automation).
- Workers in overlapping shifts or part-time schedules, to meet peak demand (a common practice of airlines, hotels, hospitals, banks, and fast-food restaurants).
- Discount pricing (weekend rates for hotels, special airfares), to increase customer demand in slack periods.
- Standard service packages, standard facility and job design, audit teams, employee and manager incentives systems, and extensive worker training, to control customer service and quality levels.
- Computer and telecommunications technology, to link geographically dispersed locations.

Participation Is In

In a knowledge economy human resources—and not financial and physical capital—are an organization's competitive edge, and management must maximize the output of highly educated workers. As the organization man becomes a dying species and workers owe their livelihoods primarily to professional training and brain power rather than membership in a business organization, participatory management styles are becoming increasingly important. The rise of the gold-collar worker is requiring a shift from an authoritarian management style to a networking, people-oriented, participatory style of management. In this system, people learn from one another horizontally, are resources for everyone else, and receive support and assistance from many different directions. Along with a change in the style of management comes a change in the emphasis in management (see box). Intuition is becoming increasingly valuable because there is an overabundance of data and judgment is needed to discriminate among competing options.

Participatory management evolves into the new ideal of self-management—employees taking responsibility and initiative, monitoring their work, using managers and supervisors as teachers and facilitators. Self-management presumes that workers are competent, self-confident, and independent and that people perform better when they manage themselves. It assumes that people want to

- Work with people who treat them with respect,
- Do interesting work,
- Be recognized for good work,
- Have a chance to develop their skills,
- Work for people who listen to ideas about how to do things better,
- Have a chance to think for themselves,
- Have an opportunity to see the results of their work,
- Work for an efficient manager,
- Work on a job that has challenge,
- Feel well informed about what is going on.

Underlying all these expectations is the fact that most workers today want more than just a paycheck from work. They want to express themselves and their values, make a difference in society, and fit work harmoniously with other priorities such as family, health, and spirituality. See table 10.1 for a comparison of the basic assumptions of the industrial and knowledge economies.

"YOU JUST DON'T UNDERSTAND"

As the numbers of women and men in the total workforce equalize, managers must understand the differences in their styles of communication. In *You Just Don't Understand: Women and Men in Conversation* Deborah Tannen, who teaches linguistics at Georgetown University, summarizes years of research. The following key differences are discussed in the book:

- Men and women use language for different purposes. Men use language to preserve their independence and maintain their position in a group, while women use language to create connections and intimacy.

- Men and women define communication differently. Men view communication as the discussion of important topics, while women view communication as establishing intimacy by sharing their concerns, their daily experiences, and their fleeting thoughts.

- Men and women communicate differently. Men tend to state their needs directly, women are more likely to be indirect—to suggest rather than demand.

- Men and women express intimacy differently. Men express intimacy through doing things together and being together; women express intimacy through conversation.

- Men and women view conflict differently. For men taking opposite sides is a basic way of doing things; women avoid conflict and taking opposite sides.

Managers who understand these differences in how men and women communicate will be better able to communicate with all people effectively.

The New Ethic: Cooperation, Not Competition

Because knowledge grows in value as it is shared, business organizations are restructuring to facilitate cooperation. The success of Japanese management methods is based in large part on their emphasis on cooperation and participation. Companies can facili-

Table 10.1 Comparison of Basic Business Assumptions in Industrial and Knowledge Economics

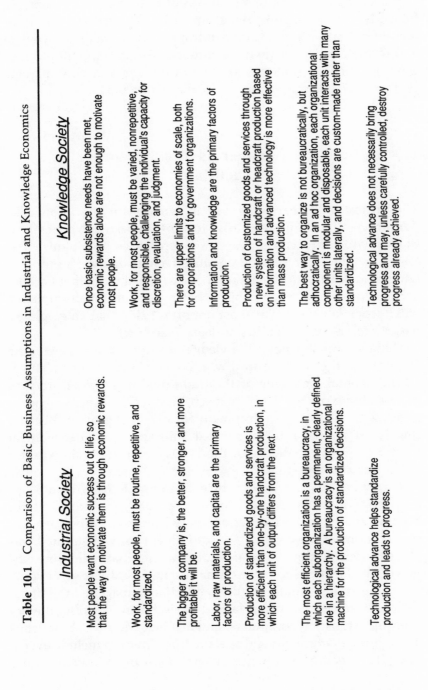

Industrial Society	*Knowledge Society*
Most people want economic success out of life, so that the way to motivate them is through economic rewards.	Once basic subsistence needs have been met, economic rewards alone are not enough to motivate most people.
Work, for most people, must be routine, repetitive, and standardized.	Work, for most people, must be varied, nonrepetitive, and responsible, challenging the individual's capacity for discretion, evaluation, and judgment.
The bigger a company is, the better, stronger, and more profitable it will be.	There are upper limits to economies of scale, both for corporations and for government organizations.
Labor, raw materials, and capital are the primary factors of production.	Information and knowledge are the primary factors of production.
Production of standardized goods and services is more efficient than one-by-one handcraft production, in which each unit of output differs from the next.	Production of customized goods and services through a new system of handcraft or headcraft production based on information and advanced technology is more effective than mass production.
The most efficient organization is a bureaucracy, in which each suborganization has a permanent, clearly defined role in a hierarchy. A bureaucracy is an organizational machine for the production of standardized decisions.	The best way to organize is not bureaucratically, but adhocratically. In an ad hoc organization, each organizational component is modular and disposable, each unit interacts with many other units laterally, and decisions are custom-made rather than standardized.
Technological advance helps standardize production and leads to progress.	Technological advance does not necessarily bring progress and may, unless carefully controlled, destroy progress already achieved.

tate cooperation by allowing groups of entrepreneurs to operate beneath a broad organizational umbrella. The theory is that by allowing creative and intuitive entrepreneurs to maintain control and responsibility for their venture the corporation will produce a more satisfied employee and new products and new markets that revitalize the company from the inside out.

The Manager as Teacher and Facilitator

The critical skill that is desired in workers in the knowledge economy is the ability to think—to synthesize, make generalizations, divide into categories, draw references, distinguish between fact and opinion, and organize facts to analyze a problem. Education must continue beyond early formal schooling because knowledge of any given subject that is not continually updated will become obsolete. The most important skill that an employee has, therefore, is the ability to learn (see box).

Managers in the new knowledge economy are teachers and facilitators who don't control workers but liberate them. This is a fundamental reshaping of the traditional managerial prerogative of giving orders. To be a coach, teacher, and mentor means creating a nourishing environment for personal growth. Because this is so contrary to traditional military-style management thinking, the big challenge of the 1990s is not to retrain workers but to retrain managers.

In a *Harvard Business Review* article in August 1990 William Wiggenhorn, Motorola Corporation's corporate vice president for training and education, described how Motorola University was created to meet the company's requirement for well-trained employees. During the 1980s, after discovering that many line employees had trouble doing basic math, could hardly read, or could not understand simple English and that management trainees with college degrees often lacked basic business skills like accounting, statistics, computers, and algebra, Motorola broadened its training program beyond specific techniques to include everything from reading and English comprehension to graduate work

PRODUCTIVITY AND PEOPLE POWER

As companies invest in high technology to improve productivity, they also must invest in the people who use the technology. The conventional wisdom among U.S. manufacturers is that improving productivity requires automating and getting rid of people. In 1990 the accounting firm Grant Thornton surveyed 250 midsize U.S. manufacturing companies on their productivity problems. Over a third thought their productivity problems were minor because they were caused by people who could be replaced by machines, leading Grant Thornton to conclude that "Manufacturers place more importance on investment in plant and equipment than on investment in people in their attempts to increase productivity." In fact, one of the accounting firm's clients spent $500,000 on a new computer system for resource planning and then found it didn't work. Grant Thornton discovered that there was nothing wrong with the machine but that the company's employees didn't know how to work the system: the company had decided to save $10,000 by not buying the vendor's training program.

---

in computer-integrated manufacturing. Motorola learned that it was more effective to provide elementary education in conjunction with local schools than to fire long-term employees for lack of basic skills.

Continual Entrepreneurship

Managers will increasingly be required to be innovators and entrepreneurs in addition to being teachers and facilitators. Control-oriented administrators will be less and less in demand. For business managers this means understanding that entrepreneurship is a form of management that shifts resources from an area of low productivity to an area of high productivity.

Entrepreneurs are not risk takers but rather opportunity takers. Peter Drucker in his book *Innovation and Entrepreneurship* describes successful entrepreneurs as people who stay with businesses they know, are good at, and like; who understand their own strengths and weaknesses; who seek out opportunities that take advantage of strengths and avoid overloading weaknesses; and who focus on the two key tasks of team building and managing cash flow. Drucker states that an entrepreneur will fail if he or she fails to perform the two key entrepreneurial management tasks:

- *Managing money:* Successful new enterprises generally reinvest all their money in innovation. They must manage liquidity and cash and ensure that the maximum sources of money are available.

- *Building top management:* Top managers should have the attitudes, chemistry, and complimentary skills that are compatible with an entrepreneurial environment. It can take several years to build an effective team of nine to eleven members.

Studies of successful entrepreneurs show that they are generally motivated by the desire for independence, challenge, achievement, and compensation (generally as an outgrowth of meeting challenges and achievement rather than as a primary focus). The same studies of successful entrepreneurs show that they are self-directed, self-nurturing, and action-oriented and have high energy levels and tolerance for uncertainty. Individuals who do not exhibit these traits will most likely fail at entrepreneurial activities. The fact that 55 percent of all new businesses fail in the first five years is evidence that large numbers of individuals lack entrepreneurial capability. Similarly, the dismal record of many large companies to establish entrepreneurial activities (Exxon's failure in office automation, for example) shows that entrepreneurial management is not easily acquired.

Successful entrepreneurs are not risk takers but rather opportunity takers who are constantly looking to shift resources—both human and financial—to areas of higher return. Successful entrepreneurs do not rely on luck to find good opportunities but systematically search for innovative opportunities, including

- A change in industry and market structure (industry can grow at 30 to 50 percent without providing significant specialization opportunity),
- A change in demographic factors,
- A change in perception by customers,

- New knowledge (knowledged-based innovation is very risky but can be very profitable if successful).

A good entrepreneurial strategy has to be market based and driven. Large companies that have been successful innovators (Proctor and Gamble, Johnson & Johnson, Bell Labs, Citicorp) are all highly disciplined and have a disciplined, market-oriented planning process. The many high-tech entrepreneurial failures generally can be traced to their engineer-founder's contempt of the market and the company's failure to be market-driven.

There are five possible alternative entrepreneurial marketing strategies:

- Be a market leader (DuPont): cut prices before competitors and stay ahead of market.
- Always be second after innovation (IBM, the Japanese): exploit market niches and the bad habits of market leaders. Bad habits include premium prices and maximizing rather than optimizing, which was Xerox's mistake with its too complex, sophisticated copiers.
- Create a market niche: if you move fast enough, no one else will get there.
- Create a skill niche (automotive electrical companies like Delco, Busche, and Catus): develop skill expertise that others can't match.
- Meet a need: change the economic characteristics of a product from your reality to your customer's reality. (This is how GE controls 90 percent of municipal lightbulb sales).

Occasionally, a genuine innovation creates users, but normally customers create the use. Innovators need to go out and question, look, listen, and ask, with particular emphasis on actual behavior, not motivation.

The Managerial Implications of the New Management Theory

Managing service companies, motivating highly skilled knowledge workers, and planning innovation and entrepreneurship will increasingly dominate business management theory and replace industrial management theory's emphasis on administration, financial management, and control. Managers will need to understand the distinctions between service and manufacturing—and learn how to motivate skilled knowledge workers, how to liberate employees' potential by increasing their participation in the management process, how to serve as a teacher and facilitator. and how to think like an entrepreneur even while working in a large organization.

The emergence of the knowledge economy also is dramatically changing the financial world facing businesspeople. The following section discusses how the knowledge economy is changing the financial system and the attractiveness of different types of investments.

III

THE EFFECT OF THE KNOWLEDGE ECONOMY ON THE FINANCIAL SYSTEM AND INVESTMENTS

11

The Financial System in Crisis and Its Future

The world financial system is experiencing a whirlwind of change: U.S. savings and loan losses seem to grow weekly; Japan has replaced the United States as the center of the world's largest banks; the U.S. securities industry doubled in size in five years with record profits and then entered a bear market with major layoffs and the failure of one of its leading players. These changes are symptomatic of the financial system's adjustment to the emerging knowledge economy. This chapter discusses the U.S. financial system, the causes of its current crisis, its future, and the role played by government in shaping the system.

Crisis in the Financial System

A growing domestic financial crisis has struck major segments of the financial system, and the regulatory scheme that supports them is showing significant strains. Commercial banks have written off billions of dollars in recent years in bad loans to domestic energy producers, real estate developers, and various corporations, while experiencing massive erosion of the system's traditional markets. Many major corporations have effectively eliminated their use of commercial banks through the issuance of commercial paper. Similarly, middle-market companies are an area of intensifying competition, as more banks (and savings and loans) seek to enter this market and as securitization of various loans allows strong players to originate a higher volume than their portfolios can absorb.

In the consumer banking arena, commercial banks find the market increasingly difficult because of increasing competition and the spread of securitization of many consumer loan categories. Nonfinancial institutions have become major players in the consumer market—General Motors Acceptance Corporation is now the largest mortgage servicer in the United States, and Ford Motor Credit one of the largest originators of mortgages—contributing to a level of domestic bank failures unequaled since the Great Depression.

The thrift industry is in even worse shape than the commercial banking system. After having suffered massive losses in the early 1980s because of negative interest spreads on portfolios of fixed-rate mortgages, the industry subsequently lost again in under-writing commercial real estate development. As a result, the thrift industry has no net worth as an industry.

In 1990 insurance companies became the next major segment of the financial system to confront serious problems. Major insurance companies like the Equitable made headlines for their losses and staff cutbacks, and estimates indicated that as much as 40 percent of the insurance industry might suffer from bad investments in junk bonds and real estate. Concerns were heightened by the realization that insurance companies were regulated by individual states and were not protected by the federal government.

Even the nation's corporate pension systems are not safe. The Pension Benefit Guarantee Corporation, which guarantees the solvency of pension funds, is suffering from reserves that are inadequate to deal with its liabilities.

In the international arena, the problems of Third World debtors pose a risk to the entire U.S. financial system. This was recognized by the commercial banking system in 1987, when it took massive reserves against its Latin American loans to compensate for possible default. The reserves taken were enough to put the entire commercial banking system in the red for the first time since the Great Depression. Moreover, additional reserves will need to be made in future years, further reducing the long-term profitability of the commercial banking system. In fact, bank loans for Latin American debtors such as Argentina, Mexico, and Brazil trade on the secondary market at prices that suggest that an amount comparable to what was charged off in 1987 will need to be charged off in the future.

The problems caused by international Third World debt are paralleled by the U.S. debt structure, particularly the debt of the federal government. Massive deficits have been generated since the beginning of the Reagan administration, federal debt has mushroomed, and for many years tax advantages have encouraged corporations to leverage themselves rather than rely on equity to support their financial needs. Individuals, as well, have incurred massive mortgage and consumer debt because tax benefits are associated with borrowing and not with saving. This high level of debt creates a rigid system that is incapable of responding to constant economic change.

Forces Creating Change in the Financial System

Three basic forces have been creating change in the financial system—deregulation of the industry by the elimination of old restrictive laws, implementation of new computer technology, and changing savings and borrowing patterns on the part of customers. Deregulation has been going on for approximately ten years, since the passage of two landmark pieces of legislation— the Depository Institutions Deregulation and Monetary Control Act of 1980 and Depository Institutions Act of 1982. Beyond these changes in its external environment because of the changing economy and society, the financial system also is participating in the technological revolution in computers and communications in its internal operating environment. This revolution is having a dual effect: it is making obsolete much past investment in technology and systems and it is creating massive overcapacity (see box).

This overcapacity was illustrated by the merger of Wells Fargo

---

AUTOMATED STOCK SELECTION:
THE RISE OF PROGRAM TRADING

Computer technology is transforming the way stock selections are being made through program trading, stock indices, and other methods. Wells Fargo Investment Advisors, the investment subsidiary of Wells Fargo Bank and one of the largest stock investors in the United States, manages its large portfolio by buying a cross-section of stocks that match market benchmarks such as the Standard & Poor's 500 Stock Index. The theory is that investments by Wells Fargo Investment Advisors will match overall market performance and large investors will slightly outpace the market because of Wells Fargo's efficiency and very low transaction costs. Wells Fargo Investment Advisors charge fees of .05 percent of assets under management compared to the 1 percent fee and higher fees that are charged by traditional advisors—a savings that reflects Wells Fargo Investment Advisors's ability to manage a stock portfolio of over $60 billion with a total staff of only 110 people.

---

and Crocker National Bank in 1985. In 1977 the two institutions employed 35,000 people; by 1987 the merged organization (Wells Fargo) employed 20,000 and held the same market share of banking business in California that the two institutions held together in 1977, even though the market in California had grown substantially over that ten-year period. The trend shown by this merger is clear: with the aid of new computer technology (like ATM networks) one person can do work that required two people ten years ago. As deregulation continues in the financial services industries and banks merge across state lines, the trend toward reduction in banking staff will become the norm.

At the same time that the industry is being transformed by a new legal structure and new technology, customers' basic needs and savings and borrowing patterns are changing. The two most significant changes are the shift from international lending to domestic lending due to the crisis in the developing countries and the shift from consumer emphasis on borrowing to an emphasis on savings. As the baby boomers of the 1950s and 1960s mature, their savings rate is anticipated to rise to an average of 12 percent of GNP by the year 2000. Artificially low interest rates for savers will be eliminated, and a larger segment of the consumer population (due to its overall aging pattern) will need increased savings for retirement and for children's education.

These two shifts—from international to domestic investment and from consumer borrowing to savings—will result in a greater availability of funds for investment in domestic industry and businesses. It also should provide an element of relief for the U.S. government deficit problems, as the pool of savings available to fund the deficit will have less competition from other sources (see box).

Major Financial Institutions in New Forms

Institutions mobilize and transmit individual savings into the global market. Both in the United States and abroad, corporate

---

LENDING FOR HUMAN CAPITAL

The biggest lending program for the creation of human capital is the guaranteed student loan program of the federal government. Currently this program has 4.1 million loans outstanding with a total value of $49 billion. Since its inception in 1965 the program has made more than 90 million loans and has been used by millions of students to pay for education and training in a wide variety of fields and occupations, from surgeons to beauticians.

The program also has spawned one of the largest and most successful financial institutions in the United States—the Student Loan Marketing Association, or Sallie Mae, as it is popularly called. Since its founding in 1972 Sallie Mae has provided additional money for student financing by purchasing loans from private lenders, using funds raised in the bond market. Its 1990 loan portfolio of $24.6 billion includes $16 billion of student loans (almost 30 percent of the total) and $8.6 billion in loans to banks that are collateralized by student loans the banks hold.

---

and nonprofit institution pension funds represent a huge aggregate of capital. Mutual funds also have shown dramatic growth in recent years, as individual investors reenter the stock market through the mutual fund vehicle as opposed to through direct ownership of stock.

Technology is playing a role in the rise of both of these types of institutions. Computer technology dramatically lowers the cost of aggregating capital and creating another layer of management for it. The whole process of issuing statements and marketing services has been dramatically simplified. Even more important, technology allows these new forms of financial institutions to act like older institutions without their disadvantages. Both mutual funds and pension funds are taking over many of the traditional roles of commercial banks and savings and loans without their disadvantages.

Pension and mutual funds, for example, require no capital to cushion against a loss of value in assets because pension and mutual funds are essentially pass-through intermediaries that do not promise their liability holders a specified return in the way that a bank or savings and loan does. Without a requirement to earn a return on capital, pension and mutual funds can pay more for earning assets than competing banks and savings and loans and still return a higher yield to their liability holders. Money market mutual funds pay shareholders more than small bank certificates of deposit even though money market funds invest in large bank certificates of deposit and other low-yielding investments like treasury bills and commercial paper.

The Future of the Financial System

These changes will affect the financial industry in three major areas—consolidation, nationwide banking, and the blurring of distinctions between different financial institutions. Consolidation of the banking industry is linked closely with the advent of nationwide banking.

From 1940 to 1980 the number of banks worldwide declined from 150,000 to 35,000, reflecting fundamental economic pressures that encourage consolidation of banking and financial systems in all countries. The number of U.S. banks, however, increased slightly, from 14,500 in 1940 to 14,700 in 1980. Regulatory restraints limited the ability of the U.S. financial services system to be consolidated, resulting in excess capacity in the banking industry and 33 percent more banks and branches than fast food outlets. In the early 1980s the consulting firm of Edward Carpenter & Associates of Los Angeles, which specialized in commercial banking, predicted that by the year 2000 the number of commercial banks in the United States would dwindle from 14,700 to 1,500. It also forecasted, however, that there would be 500,000 formal access points to those financial institutions versus the 68,000 that existed in 1982 (40,000 branch offices and 28,000 ATMs).

Nationwide banking is already becoming a reality: major financial institutions with multistate operations include Citicorp, First Interstate, North Carolina National Bank, Chemical Bank, First Nationwide Savings, and Banc One. Nationwide ATM networks and issuing of credit cards; loan production offices for corporate and commercial banking; Edge Acts for international banking; and bank holding company subsidiaries in consumer finance, commercial finance, and mortgage banking—all provide most major commercial banking institutions with some form of interstate network, even if it is not a full banking network. The expansion of ATM networks and the availability of electronic nationwide banking will grow even more dramatically in the future.

Accompanying the automation of the financial system will be its consolidation into an emerging two-tier financial system that will extinguish thousands of financial services companies. In the first tier ten to twenty giant national institutions (popularly known as megabanks) will handle most consumer financial services and large corporate banking. Many of these institutions will belong to global networks of financial services companies. In the second tier specialized financial services organizations will be primarily oriented to financing small and medium-sized businesses. Each specialized type of financial services institution also will diversify and enter fields that used to be handled by separate institutions. Leaders in this movement include American Express, Merrill Lynch, Prudential Insurance Company, Sears Roebuck, and AT&T. Merrill Lynch took in more than $50 billion in deposits in four years with its Cash Management Account—more than Citibank acquired in over 117 years. These brokerage customers represent a large source of funds and also the affluent market that most banks seek.

Companies are restructuring to facilitate the flow of information, knowledge, and entrepreneurship. The most successful financial services organizations will institutionalize a flexible entrepreneurial philosophy by smashing the managerial hierarchy or pyramid that impedes the flow of information and decision making; restructuring businesses into smaller organizational units that facilitate the flow of information; and developing incentive systems for information sharing (networks). In this new environment small banks will suffer from the loss of free funds, which historically have been one of their major competitive advantages. An opportunity to succeed exists, however, if they take advantage of their local service orientation and effectively fill specific market niches.

Government: The Guardian of the Status Quo and Its New Role

Economists and other professionals who have studied the problem predict that the regulation and structure of the financial industry will become one of the hottest political topics of the 1990s. As the Federal Deposit Insurance Corporation addresses the problems of the thrift industry and the commercial banking system, and as the Securities and Exchange Commission confronts Wall Street and the securities industry, the fear is that change can occur so fast that governmental schemes for maintaining a sound financial system will be inadequate to the task. This fear was highlighted during the stock market crash of October 1987, when the Dow Jones industrials dropped a record 20 percent in a single day. Panicked investors and the popular press speculated about whether the crash would lead into major depression, as had the stock market crash of 1929.

According to the economist Joseph Schumpeter's classic doctrine of the creative destruction of capitalism, as the financial system in the United States and the world at large creates new technology and new investment, it renders old investments obsolete and unprofitable. This dynamic pattern of creation and destruction will be the fate of substantial sectors of the financial system.

The technological revolution in banking is creating a no-win situation for the U.S. government as two opposing government policies collide. Policies encouraging efficiency and competitiveness run directly contrary to policies favoring stability and soundness of the financial system. Efficiency and competitiveness require a much higher level of failure, as inefficient and uncompetitive businesses are driven out by those who invest in ongoing technological change. Outright failures of financial institutions such as banks and S&Ls and a massive merger movement will drive inefficient firms out of business.

As the primary creditor of the bankrupt companies (through deposit insurance) the government suffers losses as inefficient, weak companies are driven into bankruptcy. There will be winners who can take advantage of the overcapacity to acquire sound assets at bargain prices—most likely new entries into the system that are not burdened with past investments as well as the best managed of existing institutions.

The transformation of the financial system and the financial services industry will require a totally new role for government, which will find it increasingly difficult to control the money supply and the interrelation of monetary and fiscal policy. For example, the commercial banking system after World War II accounted for 70 percent of the total assets of the financial services companies, by 1987 that figure had dropped to 30 percent. As commercial banks become a smaller participant in the overall financial services market and as computers and telecommunications become the central feature of the financial system, it becomes increasingly difficult to identify the money that is to be controlled. An increasingly globally linked electronic society will require whole new approaches to government management of the domestic economy as well as unprecedented levels of international cooperation to manage the global economy.

12

Securities: The Secular Bull Market

If you are an investor, you will be pleased to learn that the massive transition that the U.S. and world economies are currently undergoing should create the conditions for a long-term secular bull market. The support for a bull market will come from two sources: (1) new technologies coupled with a maturing workforce should generate a tremendous surge in productivity, lower inflation, and increase profitability, which will lift stock earnings and prices; and (2) an aging population coupled with an increase in working women should create a tremendous savings boom.

In the 1990s U.S. baby boomers will move into their primary savings years of forty to sixty, and their savings will reduce interest rates as more capital is available for new investment, which, in turn, will raise both stock and bond prices. This chapter discusses these forces as well as some specific developments in the bond market of interest to investors.

The Rise of a Global Capital Market

Investors need to understand that the world's capital markets are becoming a single, integrated global market. Historically, investment levels and interest rates in individual countries were determined by the national savings rate, investment activity, and overall governmental policy. The exception to this was the London capital market, which financed much international development in the early days of the British empire and continued to do so through the post–World War II era. Postwar New York also became a major player in international financing, but its international role was not closely tied to its domestic role.

Money is information in motion. This critical fact is shaping a global postindustrial financial system. As modern electronics eliminate the use of cash and checks as the primary monetary instruments, the speed at which information can be moved increases dramatically: it now takes eleven seconds to post a bank transaction from any part of the globe to any part of the globe. In a single global capital market money is transferred around the world at the speed of light with the touch of a computer button (see box). As interest rates and stock yields move toward a single

---

THE AUTOMATED EXCHANGE: THE STORY OF NASDAQ

NASDAQ, the Automated Exchange of the National Association of Securities Dealers, is not located in one of the three major financial centers of New York, London, or Tokyo, and yet it is the world's third largest stock market in terms of trading volume and highly likely to be the largest by the year 2000. NASDAQ does not have a trading floor, and yet it executes huge volumes of trades. This unusual stock market is essentially a computer center located in a suburb of Washington, DC.

NASDAQ operates through a network of 500 market makers who use a nationwide electronic network to negotiate the purchase and sale of shares of the 4,321 companies listed on the NASDAQ. This is almost three times the number of companies listed on the New York Stock Exchange and almost six times the number listed on the American Stock Exchange. Although many of these companies are small, young firms, 700 of NASDAQ companies could qualify for the New York Stock Exchange listings (equal to half the number of companies currently listed), and 1,800 could qualify for listing on the American Stock Exchange (equal to over twice the number currently listed). NASDAQ represents the way all stock trades will be handled in the future.

global level, global savings rates determine local interest rates. The cost of a U.S. home mortgage is directly related to the savings rate in Japan.

In this increasingly interconnected global economy new capital markets are rivaling the size and importance of the U.S. market. The most important of these are the Euromarkets centered in London and the Japanese market centered in Tokyo, but major stock markets also exist in Australia, Hong Kong, Singapore, Paris, Frankfurt, Milan, and Madrid, and minor stock markets exist in Third World countries, including South Korea, Taiwan, the Philippines, Thailand, Indonesia, India, Brazil, Mexico, Argentina, Chile, Nigeria, and Jordan. Modern communications will increasingly link these individual stock markets into an integrated global system.

Long-Wave Theory

Kondratieff wave theory postulates that the economy goes through a long-term cycle of secular growth followed by secular stagnation followed again by new secular growth that reflects the effects of new technology. The post–World War II period illustrates how high productivity and economic growth have affected the stock market: the relatively strong productivity increases of 1950s and 1960s in the United States and the world were followed by declines in the 1970s as the economy shifted out of a matured industrial economy. In 1966 the stock market had risen over a fifteen-year period to 995.15, a gain of 615 percent over a sixteen-year period, with two corrections of approximately 20 percent.

As the shift to a knowledge economy results in productivity increases and rising earnings, the stock market should experience the same long-term secular gains that were experienced in the post–World War II period. In that period large industrial companies experienced dramatic growth, reflecting the creation of a mature industrial economy. In the knowledge economy other types of companies will experience the growth and improved profitability that industrial companies in the postwar period enjoyed. In fact, a hypothetical service company index made up of thirty large blue-chip service companies such as Aetna Life and Casualty, American Express, AT&T, CitiCorp, Federal Express,

Hospital Corporation of America, McDonald's, Marriott, Merrill Lynch, and Time, Inc. dramatically outperformed the Dow Jones industrial average in the period 1964 to 1984, increasing by over 700 percent while the Dow increased less than 50 percent.

The Coming Savings Boom

Supporting the long-term secular bull market will be an overall growth in the number of stock investors and an increase in the overall savings rates, which will release more money for stock investment. The growth in stock market investors has been phenomenal. In 1952 over 6 million Americans owned stock, equivalent to 4 percent of the population; 47 million owned stock in 1985, equivalent to 20 percent of the population. In the ten-year period from 1975 to 1985 the median age of all stockholders in the United States dropped from fifty-two to forty-four years. Most saving and investment occur after age forty, so this huge pool of experienced investors moving into their prime savings years is expected to create a tremendous surge in stock buying.

In 1986 U.S. households saved only 3.9 percent of their disposable income. Although it was the worst year for personal savings since World War II, the stock market reached record highs, reflecting the growth of both institutional and individual investors. Because households provide 90 percent of net U.S. savings, the personal savings rate is critical to capital investment, interest rates, and the long-term performance of the stock market.

Demographics affect savings behavior. Between the ages of eighteen and forty-four people need to buy housing, furniture, cars, and other consumer durables, so they tend to borrow, making these years their prime borrowing years. As people age and incomes rise, they save more because they already have bought the majority of their consumer durables and because they begin to worry about their needs for retirement. The peak earning years (normally age forty-five to sixty-four) become the primary savings years. In terms of national savings patterns, the age group eighteen to forty-four borrows from the age group forty-five to sixty-four. In retirement, households save little and usually spend the income from their savings.

In the United States there will be a massive shift in the relative size of the age groups eighteen to forty-four and forty-four to sixty-five beginning around 1990, which should result in an increase in the personal savings rate. In 1960 the twenty-five to forty-four age group was approximately 30 percent larger than the forty-four to sixty-five age group. By 1990 the twenty-five to forty-four age group was approximately 75 percent larger than the forty-four to sixty-five group—seven people in their prime borrowing years for every four in their prime savings years. After 1990 the twenty-five to forty-four age group will steadily decline in size relative to the forty-four to sixty-five age group, and by the year 2010 the forty-four to sixty-five age group will actually be 5 percent larger than the twenty-five to forty-four age group. Thus there will be more people in their prime savings years than in their prime borrowing years. If this demographic shift is coupled with a reduction in the demands of the federal government on the savings pool of the country as the deficits of the Reagan years are substantially brought down or eliminated, a massive increase in capital and substantially lower interest rates will be available for investment in the United States.

Demographic trends in savings and the related effect on stock market values are reflected in the experience of Japan. The Japanese high savings rate in recent years has averaged approximately 20 percent of the country's GNP. Most economic analysts attribute these high rates to a combination of culturally reinforced thrift and encouraging government policy, but Japan's high savings rate is also a product of Japanese demographics, which in the 1980s were similar to the demographics that the United States will experience in the 1990s. The peak in the Japanese baby boom after World War II preceded the U.S. peak by about eight years, so Japan in the 1980s had a relatively high proportion of its population in the most productive and highest savings years of forty-five to sixty-four. The result was very high levels of productivity increases for Japan and a high savings rate with correspondingly low interest rates and a stock market boom. Between 1978 and 1988 the yield on Japanese government bonds fell from 9 to 3.5 percent, with a resulting tripling in the market value of the bonds with 1978 interest rates. Other Japanese investments such as corporate stocks and bonds and real estate showed greater gains than government bonds.

Investing in the Future

The driving force in the evolution of the knowledge economy is new technology, which for investors represents both an opportunity and a risk. Investing in the early stages of a technological breakthrough or in the commercialization of a new technology can provide tremendous returns, but the development path of new technology is always uncertain. The investment landscape is littered with companies that failed because new technology did not develop in the way that was expected.

Social and demographic trends generally present less opportunity and risk than technology does. Those trends can be predicted more easily than the evolution of new technology. For example, the aging of the population in the U.S. and other advanced countries is a trend that is well established and unlikely to be reversed, allowing investors to predict with a low degree of risk that industries such as health care will grow as the population ages (see box).

As the world economy develops into a single integrated economy, there are two compelling reasons to invest globally: (1) global investing provides greater diversification for the investor, and diversification is a primary means of reducing risk in an investment portfolio; and (2) many overseas markets provide potentially greater returns than those available in the U.S. market. During the 1980s the Japanese stock market outperformed

---

NURSING HOMES: A GROWTH INDUSTRY

In 1990 nursing homes were a major industry, with 1.7 million residents and $50 billion in revenues, and they soon will become one of the country's premier growth industries. In the sixty-year period from 1990 to 2050 the U.S. population is expected to increase by 20 percent. In the same period, the population of U.S. nursing homes is projected to almost quadruple to approximately 5.4 million. The United States will have to build a 100-bed nursing home every day during the decade 1990 to 2000 to house the growing nursing home population.

---

the U.S. market by a wide margin, and in the 1990s European stock markets are expected to outperform the U.S. market as a result of the reunification of Germany, the continuing integration of the EEC, and the conversion of Eastern Europe to open-market economies.

There are two alternative ways to invest globally—directly in the individual stocks of foreign companies, which is increasingly easy to do with major European and Japanese companies since many are listed on major U.S. exchanges through the mechanism of ADRs, or in mutual funds that do non-U.S. investing. The three types of mutual funds for international investing are global investment funds that invest anywhere in the world that they believe provides an investment opportunity, regional funds that focus on a specific region of the world (such as Merrill Lynch's extremely successful Pacific Fund), and individual country funds (such as the Japan Fund, the Germany Fund, and the Mexico Fund) (see box).

The Rise of the Junk Bond Market

The rise of junk bonds was a major development in U.S. capital markets during the 1980s and will eventually dominate the total bonds outstanding as investment-grade bonds shrink as a percentage of total bonds outstanding.

There is a relationship between the change in the economy and the growth of junk bonds. A *high-yield bond*—which is the more

---

BIG PROFITS FOR GLOBAL INVESTORS

Investors who invested outside the United States in the 1980s probably did very well. Even though the U.S. stock market experienced one of its greatest bull markets, its stocks ranked only fourteenth globally in their ten-year rate of return. Some of the countries that exceeded the 153 percent ten-year rate of return of the U.S. market included Sweden (870%), Japan (529%), Italy (313%), West Germany (248%), and France (218%).

---

formal term for the junk bond—is any bond that is considered noninvestment grade. Bonds are simply loans made by investors (usually large institutions) to a company that is raising capital to construct buildings, purchase new equipment, hire more personnel, or perform research and development for new technology and products. The borrower (the bond issuing company) promises the lender (the bond holder) to repay the principal of that loan at a future date and to pay interest until that date—essentially like a long-term installment loan. Bonds sold publicly have traditionally been rated and priced according to their risk relative to treasury bonds: top-rated bonds pay the lowest rates to their buyers (closest to treasury bonds); bonds that are perceived to be riskier pay higher rates.

The two major rating services—Moody's and Standard & Poor's—rate bonds according to traditional criteria such as credit history, assets, financial strength, and sizes and sources of historical and current revenue. Standard & Poor's ratings, for example, range from AAA for bonds issued by well-established companies like AT&T, IBM, or General Motors, followed by AA, A, BBB, B, and so on down. By convention, bonds with a rating of BBB and higher are called investment grade, and those rated BB or lower are called *noninvestment grade*—or more popularly, junk. Historically, *noninvestment grade* bonds were limited to bonds previously issued by companies that had been in good standing at the time of issuance but subsequently fell into financial difficulty. Major companies like Chrysler and Ford have had their bonds downgraded at points in their history to noninvestment grade because of their financial difficulties.

The shift from an industrial economy to a new knowledge economy has introduced new kinds of issuers of noninvestment grade bonds—new, smaller service companies with a strong knowledge base. Historically, the public debt market has been closed to all but a limited number of large companies. In fact, currently, fewer than 800 companies qualify for an investment grade rating. Even though 22,000 U.S. companies have sales of $25 million or more, most of these companies do not qualify for an investment grade rating because of their smaller size, lack of credit history, or capital structure.

Traditionally, the only source of long-term debt financing for noninvestment grade companies was long-term loans from insurance companies or banks. When fixed-rate, long-term loans from banks virtually disappeared in the mid-1970s, junk bonds created a new financing mechanism that probably accelerated the process of creating the knowledge economy by doing away with the significant advantage in raising funds that large companies have long enjoyed.

The growth in the junk bond market has been dramatic. From 1978 to 1986 the market grew from $1.5 billion in bonds outstanding to an estimated $40 billion. Noninvestment-grade bonds now account for more than 21 percent of the corporate bond market, and almost all major investment banks have become active in this market. The historically high default rate of 3 percent for junk bonds means that investors will have to be selective, but this market will not dry up. Instead, the market may offer long-term contrarian investors one of their most attractive opportunities because of the steep discounts associated with many junk bond issues.

Securitization: Bonds Unlimited

Loan securitization or structured securitized credit is a hybrid form of financing that combines features of the traditional credit and securities systems. Securitization occurs when loans held by a financial institution are combined in a form that allows debt securities to be created from the loans. A key element of loan or credit securitization is separating two risks—the credit risk of the securities purchased and the credit risk of the corporation or financial institution originating the loans. Buyers of securitized loans expect cash flow from the loans (plus any credit-enhancement features) to cover expected losses and support the debt service of the securities and do not become involved with the credit quality of the corporation or financial institution originating the loans (see box).

Securitization of loans made by banks and other financial institutions began in 1970 when the recently created Government National Mortgage Association (GNMA) offered investors interest in pools of FHA and VA mortgages through the sale of a defined security. The market for mortgage-backed securities grew

COMPUTERS AND THE GROWTH OF
FINANCIAL SERVICE PRODUCTS

The result of the application of computer technology to the securities and financial markets has been an explosion in investment products, investment information, and investment complexity. Since the 1970s investors can choose from newly introduced financial products such as asset management accounts, money market funds, options and futures of all kinds, floating rate notes, zero coupon bonds, guaranteed investment contracts, universal life insurance, and a wide range of securitized loans (which could not have been developed without the computer).

rapidly, and by 1985 mortgage-backed securities represented the second largest pool of securities outstanding after U.S. government securities. In 1987 new mortgage-backed securities issues (both public and private) represented about two-thirds of all mortgage originations, and the total volume of mortgage-backed securities outstanding grew to $750 billion.

Until 1985 securitization of loans was confined principally to residential mortgages. The market changed dramatically in March 1985 when the first public securitized transaction of non-mortgage assets was offered by Sperry Rand Corporation and its investment banker, First Boston. Marine Midland Bank, in conjunction with Salomon Brothers, then securitized $60 million of automobile loan receivables in May 1985, and the feasibility of securitizing nonmortgage assets was clearly established. Automobile loans were followed by the securitization of credit card loans and a wide range of other loans. By the end of 1987 securitization of nonmortgage assets had reached an annual level of $10 billion, and asset-based securities were backed by a wide range of loans, including loans on boats and recreational vehicles, airplane leases, unsecured personal loans, and life insurance policy loans. There also is $600 billion of commercial loans and $500 billion of consumer debt that potentially could be securitized. With the securitization of all types of domestic bank and thrift loans, as well as the planned securitization of large portions of international bank loans, this market could easily grow to $500 billion or $1 trillion by the early 1990s.

13

Analyzing Companies in the Knowledge Economy

Stock investment decisions in the emerging knowledge economy will be difficult because the factors that lead to corporate success are different than they have been historically. In the industrial economy (as has been discussed throughout this book) the keys to success were physical and financial capital, and economies of scale gave companies distinct competitive advantages. In the knowledge economy the keys to success are human capital and knowledge, and companies may suffer from diseconomies of scale as bureaucracy impedes knowledge and information flow and slows responsiveness. Because human capital and knowledge are hard to quantify, investment analysis becomes increasingly complex.

Benjamin Graham and Value Investing

Investing was complex in the industrial economy as well, but methods were developed over time that guaranteed an effective practitioner successful long-term results. The most consistently successful method was value investing. Benjamin Graham, author of *Security Analysis* (the Bible of security analysis) and the best-selling guide for the general public, *The Intelligent Investor,* provided the defensive investor with criteria to use in selecting common stock for purchase that offered a margin of safety as well as above-average performance. Investors such as Warren Buffett, a Graham disciple, and academic research have shown that Benjamin Graham's criteria consistently applied could have generated above-average returns during the period of the mature industrial society in the United States (1950–1975). Graham's criteria as listed in the final edition of *The Intelligent Investor* were as follows:

1. *Adequate Size of the Enterprise*
   All our minimum figures must be arbitrary and especially in the matter of size required. Our idea is to exclude small companies which may be subject to more than average vicissitudes especially in the industrial field. (There are often good possibilities in such enterprises but we do not consider them suited to the needs of the defensive investor.) Let us use round amounts: not less than $100 million of annual sales for an industrial company and not less than $50 million of total assets for a public utility.

2. *A Sufficiently Strong Financial Condition*
   For industrial companies current assets should be at least twice current liabilities—a so-called two-to-one current ratio. Also, long-term debt should not exceed the net current assets (or "working capital"). For public utilities the debt should not exceed twice the stock equity (at book value).

3. *Earnings Stability*
   Some earnings for the common stock in each of the past ten years.

4. *Dividend Record*
   Uninterrupted payments for at least the past 20 years.

5. *Earnings Growth*
   A minimum increase of at least one-third in per-share earnings in the past ten years using three-year averages at the beginning and end.

6. *Moderate Price/Earnings Ratio*
   Current price should not be more than 15 times average earnings of the past three years.

7. *Moderate Ratio of Price to Assets*
   Current price should not be more than 1½ times the book value last reported. However, a multiplier of earnings below

15 could justify a correspondingly higher multiplier of assets. As a rule of thumb we suggest that the *product* of the multiplier times the ratio of price to book value should not exceed 22.5. (This figure corresponds to 15 times earnings and 1½ times book value. It would admit an issue selling at once 9 times earnings and 2.5 times asset value, etc.)

These criteria were intended to guarantee that the defensive investor could obtain a minimum of *quality* in the past performance and current financial position of the company and a minimum of *quantity* in terms of earnings and assets per dollar of price. In his approach to value investing, Graham emphasized that the intrinsic asset value of a company provided a margin of safety and ensured that the investor was not overpaying for uncertain future earnings. If human capital and knowledge and not physical and financial resources are increasingly the intrinsic value of a company, then Graham's value-based investing approach will become obsolete as the economy moves further toward a knowledge services orientation.

Putting Human Capital on the Balance Sheet

The industrial economy shaped not only Benjamin Graham's investing approach but also standard accounting rules. Even though an economy's greatest resource is its human capital, standard accounting rules assign no value to human resources when developing the balance sheet for a business. Table 13.1 shows a balance sheet adjusted to perform financial analysis in a knowledge economy. The restated knowledge economy balance sheet includes the key resources that make a company successful in a knowledge economy environment—knowledge in the form of intellectual property and well-educated, highly skilled people.

Knowledge in the form of intellectual property is often found on the balance sheet, usually in the form of capitalized research and development expenses or the price paid to acquire a specific piece of intellectual property such as a license to use a patent. It is also found in the form of goodwill when an acquiring company

Table 13.1   Knowledge Economy Balance Sheet

Assets	Liabilities

Financial assets:
  Cash
  Accounts receivable
 	
  Securities
	Short-term liabilities:
	  Accounts payable
	  Bank loans, and commercial
	    papers
	  Long-term debt due within one
	    year

Physical assets:
  Inventory
  Plant and equipment
	Long-term liabilities:
	  Bonds
	  Term bank loans
	  Capitalized equipment losses

Intangible assets:
  Patents and copyrights
  Licenses
 	
  Formulas
 	
  Know-how
  Goodwill
	Equity:
	  Preferred stock
	  Common stock and retained
	    earnings
	  Unrecognized equity in
	    off–balance-sheet intangible assets
	    and human capital assets

Human capital assets:
  Capitalized salaries wages,
    benefits, and pension rights	

Total assets	Total liabilities and equity

pays more than book value because of market reputation or valuable know-how that the acquisition possesses.

Historically, management and analysts acknowledged the importance of employees and then ignored human capital in analysis of the financial strength and performance of companies because there was no way to quantify it. However, economists now have a method for quantifying human capital that can be included in the financial analysis of a company.

In the book titled *Investment Markets* (discussed in chapter 2) Roger Ibbotson (professor of finance at Yale's School of Management) and Gary Brinson (president of First Chicago Investment Advisors) capitalized the return to labor in the free world to estimate the percentage of wealth attributable to human capital and the percentage attributable to physical and financial capital. Just as Brinson and Ibbotson capitalized the percentage of a country's national income to develop a total sum of human capital for a country, a company's human capital can be estimated by capitalizing the return to employees. Adding back this capitalized human capital to a company's balance sheet will give a picture of its total resources and more accurately analyze the significance of human capital to the company.

Figure 13.1 shows the results of a study I performed for this book. In it I capitalized human capital for over 100 major companies in the U.S. manufacturing and service industries. As these graphs show, the largest resource by far for most companies in most industries is human capital, not physical and financial capital: approximately 70 percent of the resources of U.S. business show up nowhere on the current balance sheets. Appendix A summarizes the results of the study and its methodology.

The Link between Human Resource Management and Financial Performance

Studies conducted during the 1980s have clearly demonstrated a direct correlation between a company's management of its human resources and its financial performance:

- *The Schuster Report: The Proven Connection Between People and Profits* by Frederick E. Schuster surveyed 592 large industrial and service companies and found that companies with progressive employment policies consistently tended to do better than companies without similar policies.
- "Socially Responsible Inventing: The Financial and Socio/ Economic Issues," a study conducted for Dean Witter Reynolds by Theodore A. Bunn and Thomas Van Dyck, found that from 1981 to 1985 average compounded total return on investment for the companies listed in the book *100 Best Companies to Work for in America* was 17.69 percent more than

Figure 13.1 Capitalized Human Capital in U.S. Manufacturing and Services Industries

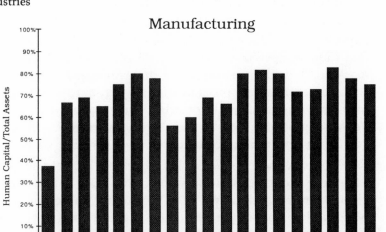

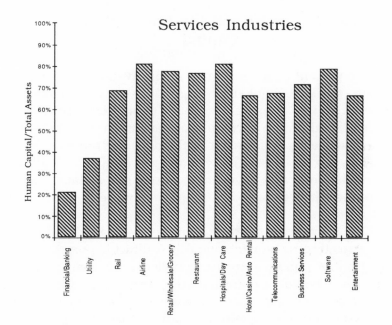

Source: Public data of companies included in study discussed in appendix A.

the average for the S&P 500 and had a stock price increase three times the average for the S&P 500.

- *People and Productivity: The New York Stock Exchange Guide to Financial Incentives and the Quality of Work Life* by William C. Freund and Eugene Epstein surveyed 1,158 companies for the New York Stock Exchange and found that three-quarters reported that human resource programs ranging from formal training, profit sharing, and quality circles to employee attitude surveys, suggestion systems, and flexible workhours were successful in improving productivity and lowering costs.

- *The Human Resource Revolution* by Dennis J. Kravetz surveyed 150 large companies from among the 1,000 largest in the United States and found that the higher these companies were ranked in human resource progressiveness the better their long-term performance.

The research shows that effective use of human resources leads to superior financial performance.

Value Investing in the Era of Human Capital

Because 70 percent of the resources of the average company are its human capital, it is not surprising that better management of these resources will improve a company's financial performance. Moreover, identification of companies that effectively use human resources can help predict superior financial performance in the future. This logic exposes the weakness in Benjamin Graham's classic model for value investing: it does not address human capital or the role of knowledge except very indirectly in earnings performance.

Evaluating a company's external environment and its competitive edge relating to human capital is a difficult process as the economy shifts rapidly into the knowledge economy. Beyond focusing on revenues, earnings, market share, and number and size of competitors, investors can assess the company generally and the company's competitive position, human capital, and management. Companies that are best positioned with the key competitive resources of knowledge and information are most likely to prosper and have good earnings and cash flow (see box). It also is important to recognize that future performance may be radically different from past performance and that long-term forecasts based on historical performance may be of little value as conditions change. A quantitative model that evaluates a company's intrinsic value in a knowledge economy must be developed in the same way that Benjamin Graham developed a quantitative model to evaluate a company's intrinsic value in an industrial economy.

Appendix B at the end of this book presents a preliminary idea of a model for analyzing companies in the knowledge economy. The purpose of this risk assessment guide is to identify companies that are either high risk or low risk because of their relative vulnerability to the emerging knowledge economy and to further qualify high-potential, undervalued companies that have been preliminarily identified by the Benjamin Graham quantitative model.

SMART INVESTORS THINK SMALL

As more and more Americans are starting their own businesses in the knowledge economy, investors have more opportunities to invest in new ventures or small businesses. Such investing is significantly different from traditional equity investing. Most new companies today are low-tech service companies and are financed by personal savings, personal loans from friends or relatives, and cash flow from jobs or spouse's job. Less than one-quarter of new ventures are financed by institutional sources. Since most new venture financing is personal, investing in the right small business or new venture can be very rewarding financially. According to a study conducted at the University of Southern California, since the early 1960s investors in small companies have done far better than those who invested in larger firms: $1 invested in 1963 in a firm with less than $5 million in capital would by 1980 have increased to about $46, but the return on $1 invested in companies with over $1 billion in capital would have been only $4.

Wal-Mart versus Sears: A Case Study

Sears, Roebuck and Wal-Mart provide a good comparison of how human capital affects the financial performance of major corporations. These companies are currently the first- and second-largest retailers in the United States, respectively, but their growth and profitability have differed markedly over the last twenty years. Sears has shown very low growth, mediocre profitability, and lacklustre stock market performance, while Wal-Mart has shown dramatic growth, huge increases in profitability, and spectacular stock market performance, making it one of Wall Street's darlings.

In the early 1970s Sears, Roebuck was one of the legends of U.S. business history. Founded in 1886 Sears had prospered with the growth of the country. Its famous mail-order catalog gave farmers access to goods that traditionally had been available only in big cities. After World War II its department stores served the needs of suburbanites, and by 1972 Sears's merchandising success had propelled it into being "the world's largest store" and a major U.S. institution: its gross sales in 1972 equaled 1 percent of the U.S. GNP; its retailing market share accounted for over 7 percent of total U.S. sales; two of every three Americans shopped at Sears within any three months; and more than half the households in the U.S. contained a Sears credit card. Its national institution status was confirmed again and again by consumer surveys, which showed that Sears was the most trusted economic institution in the country.

Founded in 1962 in Bentonville, Arkansas, Wal-Mart in 1972 had been a public company for only two years and had a small number of stores in small towns in the southeastern United States. No one considered it a significant competitor of any of the national retailing chains, such as Sears, Woolworth's, or Penney's. By 1989, however, that situation had changed dramatically. Wal-Mart's 1,300 discount stores had sales of almost $20 billion. Its one-stop family shopping stores had become the town center for small towns across the country. It had become the third-largest retailer in the United States even though it had no stores in the prime urban areas of the Pacific Coast or the Northeast, and industry growth projections showed Wal-Mart becoming the largest retailer in the country by the early 1990s, surpassing Sears. Investors in Wal-Mart stock had done very well. A $1,000 investment in Wal-Mart's initial public offering in 1970 was worth $500,000 in 1989.

While Wal-Mart was experiencing spectacular success, Sears was floundering. Starting in 1972 Sears began to experience substantial difficulty in its retailing business. Sales and profits stagnated, and its market share declined. From 1980 to 1987 Sears's merchandise sales growth was one-half the average for the retailing industry, and its share of the general U.S. merchandise market declined from 7.2 to 5.8 percent. During the 1970s and 1980s Sears tried various tactics to shore up its retailing business. It upgraded its fashion lines, added more brand name goods, and remodeled its stores, but nothing seemed to work. To cut costs, major reductions were made in the Sears workforce, including the first layoffs by Sears since the Great Depression, but its costs in 1988 were still the highest in the retailing industry. Sears overhead accounted for 32 percent of each sales dollar compared to 23 percent for K-Mart (the second largest retailer) and 17 percent for Wal-Mart.

By 1988 securities analysts began to speculate about a corporate takeover of Sears because of its modest earnings and its low stock price. Responding to this speculation, Sears announced a major corporate restructuring in October 1988—cutting corporate overhead, selling some nonconsumer-oriented businesses, selling its 110-story Chicago headquarters, and initiating a major stock repurchase. In March 1989 Sears announced a further restructuring that organized its merchandising business around six product lines and cut 800 managerial positions out of a total of 7,700.

Given Sears's market position at the beginning of the 1970s, its subsequent problems and Wal-Mart's success are remarkable. An analysis of Wal-Mart's success shows that it is based on two key factors—its effective use of employees (the company's human capital) and of modern computer and communication technology. Wal-Mart emphasizes motivating its employees and developing a long-term partnership with them. Employees are called *associates* and are kept informed about all aspects of the business. The company's founder, Sam Walton, travels extensively to keep in touch with all the stores. The following quotes from Wal-Mart's 1988 annual report summarize Wal-Mart's personnel philosophy:

- Sharing information, all of it, permits the smart application of the very best ideas and hard work of each individual. An environment of open-door communication provides for the free flow of ideas from every possible source and their appropriation throughout the Company, not just in a single department, store or division.

- Our objective is straight forward: we want each associate to have the opportunity to maximize their contribution and excel.

- What a difference our people make!

Wal-Mart focuses on using its critical resource—human capital—effectively, but it also uses computer and communications technology to improve the effectiveness of its people and the efficiency of its operations. A major part of the of the Wal-Mart program is technology designed to expedite the customer's shopping trip. All new Wal-Marts are equipped with scanner cash registers. Hand-held computers assist Wal-Mart associates in ordering merchandise in all stores. Backroom computers link each store with the Bentonville, Arkansas, general office and with various distribution centers for communications and the quick replacement of merchandise.

For faster communications with its branches, Wal-Mart maintains a six-channel television satellite system that allows headquarters executives to communicate directly with all 1,300 stores. In addition to direct communications, the TV satellite system is used to gather store data for the master computer so that Wal-Mart headquarters has daily reports from all 1,300 stores within ninety minutes of closing, to give credit card approvals in five seconds, to track the company's complex distribution system, and to share merchandising information throughout the system (for example, all 1,300 stores are shown simultaneously how to display new items). This is standard retailing and business technology, but Wal-Mart uses it more intensively than its competitors. If you had used the risk assessment guide to evaluate Wal-Mart and Sears at the beginning of 1980, Wal-Mart would have been a much lower risk than Sears in the emerging knowledge economy and a much better investment value. Consistent use of Benjamin Graham's principles coupled with an analysis implementing the philosophy contained in the risk assessment guide should give good investment results in the 1990s.

14

Real Estate and the Knowledge Economy: Opportunities in New Places

Most Americans have made some form of real estate investment—a home, a vacation home, rental property, or units in a real estate limited partnership—which gives them a strong interest in the long-term outlook for real estate. Real estate prices soared during the 1970s and the first half of the 1980s but have been declining in many parts of the United States over the last few years. The savings and loans and the commercial banks also have experienced real estate problems. Real estate, like other types of investments, is in turmoil as new knowledge-based companies create jobs and declining old industrial companies eliminate jobs and as new computer and communications technology changes the advantages, disadvantages, and economics of the city versus the suburbs and small town.

The most important overall trend that investors need to understand is that real estate is entering a secular bear market just as securities are entering a secular bull market. The cause of this is long-term demographic change. Three additional trends affecting real estate are dispersion due to technology, inflation due to the knowledge economy's emergence, and changing locational demand due to lifestyle changes. Each trend operates separately, and when they interact, they can create massive turmoil in real estate values. This chapter examines the effects of these trends on residential and commercial real estate.

Baby Bust and the End of the Housing Boom

In the two decades between 1970 and 1990 the United States experienced tremendous inflation in housing: the median price of a house nationwide and average rents quadrupled, and in some markets, such as southern California, the median price of a home increased far more. Most of this dramatic increase in the price of housing occurred between 1970 and 1985, and after 1985 housing prices continued to soar in selected markets like Southern California but in much of the country began to level off. In some markets, such as New England and the Northeast Corridor, prices declined, much to the dismay of homeowners.

The entry of the baby boomers into their prime home-buying years, coupled with a population rise, significantly affected housing prices, but the more fundamental cause is that society shifted from the nuclear family as the primary economic (and housing) unit to the individual as the primary economic (and housing) unit. This shift increased the demand for housing. As housing prices skyrocketed in the period from 1970 to 1985, more than 24 million new housing units were constructed, increasing the housing stock by almost one-third. This rate of increase in the housing stock was twice that for the population (which increased 17 percent from 1970 to 1985) but it was not enough to satisfy the demand for housing and to stabilize housing prices.

Demand for housing exploded even as the housing industry was increasing the housing stock by a third because of the rapid increase in the number of households and the rise of the two-income family. These two trends affected housing prices far more than the entry of the baby boomers into the housing market or general population growth. From 1970 to 1985 the number of households increased 40 percent compared with the 17 percent population rise because people stayed single longer, existing marriages dissolved and were not replaced with new marriages, and the population was aging. During that period the percentage of singles in their prime marrying years doubled, and the average age of first marriages increased by almost three years for both men and women. Similarly, the divorce rate for first marriages increased, reaching 50 percent in the 1970 to 1980 period, where it has remained, while the remarriage rate for both men and women declined. The rate was even higher for some age groups: in 1985 the U.S. Census Bureau forecasted that 60 percent of the first marriages for women thirty-five to thirty-nine at that time would eventually end in divorce. "The graying of America" also has increased households: in 1890, 67 percent of those over sixty-five lived with relatives; by 1985, 84 percent were living alone.

The most important factor behind the housing price increase over the last twenty years is not the trend toward more numerous households, however, but is the increase in potential mortgage credit available because of women's increasing earnings and purchasing power. From 1965 to 1985 the percentage of women in the workforce doubled, and this dramatic increase in earnings combined with improved access to mortgage credit as a result of the Equal Credit Act of 1974 have produced the dramatic increases in housing prices.

Whether residential real estate will appreciate, flatten out, or depreciate depends on a number of factors. The first factor is location: residential real estate will continue to be most influenced by trends in local economies, and rapidly growing local economies will have rising real estate prices even when most of the country doesn't. The second factor is general demographic trends: fewer first-time home buyers will have a negative effect, but more numerous and smaller households could have a positive impact by increasing demand. The third factor is government policy. Lower tax rates reduce the tax incentive for owning a home while decreased tax incentives for rental housing (which reduce supply and increase the price of rental housing) increase the demand by increasing the cost of renting.

The long-term outlook for residential real estate prices is unclear and highly dependent on the local situation, but the massive appreciation of the 1970s and first half of the 1980s will not be repeated. Those price increases were a one-time event, reflecting the transition to the knowledge economy, which created unusual demand pressures that will not be repeated.

Commercial Real Estate:
Cash Flow Counts

Currently, the United States is plagued with an oversupply of commercial real estate. The nationwide vacancy rate for office space, in fact, is approximately 20 percent. From 1970 to 1985 commercial real estate experienced even more dramatic increases in supply than residential real estate, and the square footage of occupied office buildings and gross leasable space in shopping centers more than doubled even though the U.S. population increased only 17 percent. Similarly, in the ten-year period between 1975 and 1985, the number of available hotel rooms increased 50 percent from 1.7 million to 2.6 million while average room rates increased 143 percent from $22.15 per day to $53.91 per day.

Such clear overbuilding of real estate occurred because the changing economy altered temporarily the demand pattern for commercial real estate, misleading investors and builders about long-term demand. Misguided tax incentives, designed to stimulate real estate development to meet a temporary surge in demand, further reinforced this mistake. As women joined the workforce in record numbers, almost all the job growth was in white-collar knowledge service sectors such as computers, medicine, accounting, law, education, finance, insurance, real estate, and government. From 1970 to 1985 there was a 45 percent increase in white-collar jobs as more than 22 million white-collar jobs were added to the economy.

This tremendous growth in white-collar jobs (which are generally housed in office buildings) fueled the massive increase in office space. Lenders and investors, recognizing the increasing demand for office space and stimulated by favorable tax laws, channeled excessive capital into the office building market. Similarly, shopping center growth exceeded population growth as a result of greater discretionary income, an increasingly discrete, segmented market, and the center's new role as a major social and recreational center in a period of dual-income families and large numbers of singles. Large regional malls emerged as an increasingly significant factor in the retailing environment, with a tripling in the number of centers of a million-plus square feet.

The substantial growth of hospitality and leisure properties, such as hotels, motels, restaurants, and special-purpose entertainment buildings, reflected a burgeoning population, changing lifestyles, and rising demand for entertainment fueled by the increasing income of dual-job families and affluent singles. The jump in room availability and rates reflected both an increase in the amount of travel for business and pleasure and increasing specialization in the hotel market. Similarly, restaurants grew at a faster rate than population, reflecting the large share of the food dollar being spent on eating out, due to the affluence and time pressures of dual-income couples and working singles.

What is the long-term outlook for commercial real estate in the changing economy? The 1990s will be a very bad time for commercial real estate. The current oversupply of many types of commercial real estate will take several years to be absorbed by a growing economy. Eventually, diminished tax incentives and the current oversupply will reduce the amount of new commercial development entering the market until the market comes into balance. In the interim, smart investors will pay close attention to current cash flow in evaluating commercial real estate (see box).

Dispersion: Technology and the Wide Open Spaces

For the last couple of decades in the United States, population has tended to disperse throughout the country, creating a low level of urbanization across great portions of the country. This pattern of dispersion is a reversal of the great migration to urban centers that characterized the industrial period from the end of the Civil War to the beginning of the Vietnam War (approximately 1865 to 1965). During this period, Americans migrated from farms and rural areas to large cities in successive waves, in search of work and a better life. To this group was added a stream of immigrants from Europe, who contributed to the creation of the great urban centers of the Northeast and Midwest.

In 1870 only 20 percent of the U.S. population lived in urban

---

REAL ESTATE BECOMES A GLOBAL MARKET

Historically, real estate markets were almost exclusively local markets. Buyers and sellers of real estate were local people, and the financing of real estate was handled by local institutions. Some regional and national investment funding flowed into real estate through the medium of the mortgage banker, who worked primarily with major insurance companies located in the eastern United States, but this was the exception to the rule.

In the 1980s new computer and communications technology changed this situation dramatically. Real estate markets—both in terms of the buying and selling of property and the financing of property—became national and international in scope. Major commercial properties such as office buildings and hotels in large U.S. cities like Los Angeles, San Francisco, Chicago, Washington, and New York were routinely the subject of international business transactions as buyers from Europe, the Middle East, Asia, and Latin America increasingly invested in U.S. real estate. Individual investors in the United States increasingly owned interests in apartments, office buildings, and shopping centers that they had never seen in areas of the country that they had never visited through the mechanism of the public and private limited partnership. Real estate in the future will be global.

---

areas with more than 8,000 inhabitants. By 1900 that percentage had increased to 33 percent, and by 1920, 50 percent. From 1860 to 1910 New York City's population increased 400 percent while Chicago's (the second largest city) increased 2,000 percent (from 109,000 to 2.2 million). The number of cities with populations between 10,000 and 250,000 increased from 161 in 1870 to 538 in 1910.

Between 1910 and the end of World War II the large cities of the the Northeast and the Midwest continued to grow, but the cities of the Southern and Western sunbelt began to grow dramatically. The fastest growing was Los Angeles, which built on its base of aerospace manufacturing and entertainment industries, followed by other sunbelt cities like Houston, Dallas, Atlanta, and Miami.

Then after 1965 the pattern of urbanization began to change

and Americans migrated away from large cities to smaller cities, rural areas, and the less concentrated urban areas of the South and West. During the period from 1970 to 1980 the population of towns of between 10,000 and 50,000 grew 30 percent, versus a 1.9 percent growth for cities of over 100,000. Similarly, in the same period twenty-seven of the fifty largest cities lost population and only twenty-three gained; cities losing population were 2.5 times as dense as those gaining. This trend can be expected to continue in the future as improving communications make proximity to work less important and people seek more space and lower land values for housing.

Another development that will affect the demand for residential real estate and commercial office space is the trend for people to work in their homes. Sophisticated computer and communications technology is allowing people in a wide range of occupations from literary agent to attorney to real estate broker to avoid the expense and daily grind of commuting to an office. Moreover, working at home is no longer confined to independent entrepreneurs as large organizations such as financial institutions and large law firms allow some employees to stay home part of the time or all of the time and telecommute to work. Some estimate that 25 percent of the labor force will be working at home by the year 2000 as technology improves and telecommuting becomes more widespread. This trend toward telecommuting will dramatically change housing and office patterns. Houses will be relatively larger as more people require space for offices in their homes and the demand for office space, particularly in hard-to-reach central cities, will drop. Prices for large houses that can double as homes and offices will increase and prices for commercial office space will decrease.

Inflation and the Knowledge Economy

Real estate prices fluctuate, but the basic long-term trend in U.S. real estate is upward because of inflation and population growth. Although the United States currently appears to be experiencing some deflation, the long-term trend has been steady inflation—a result of the growth in the general money supply. Concomitantly, population growth puts upward pressure on land prices as a growing population competes for fixed amounts of land. Will Rogers summed up the impact of population growth with his famous line, "Buy land—they ain't making any more of the stuff."

Local economies can be affected dramatically as certain jobs disappear and new ones appear. In Boston from 1970 to 1980 real estate values languished as the region's traditional industries, such as textiles and shoemaking, disappeared. Real estate values soared in the 1980s, however, reflecting the emergence of a dynamic high-tech and knowledge services economy that fed on Boston's position as a center of higher education. Finally, real estate values declined again at the end of the 1980s, reflecting a downturn in the region's high-tech economy and in demand from first-time homebuyers as a result of high prices and the region's static population growth. Similarly, the Midwest has languished as a result of the demise of its traditional industrial base but now appears to be undergoing a revival.

Location and Lifestyle

In cluster living unrelated individuals reside in professionally managed complexes and share support services. Such residences for single people, including those with children, may become common. Big suburban homes will become dinosaurs. As industries and technologies are developed around women who leave homemaking for jobs, food preparation will become more convenient and eating out will continue as a trend. Leisure will take on new emphasis, and home entertainment will flourish. Much of this leisure activity may be educationally oriented.

As the knowledge economy evolves, jobs will increasingly flow to the location of a critical resource—skilled, educated people. Unlike in the industrial era, when people flowed to jobs in towns located near critical natural resources like coal or iron or in big cities that were centers of manufacturing, in the knowledge economy jobs will increasingly flow to where skilled, educated people want to live—usually in areas that provide a high-quality physical environment, educational and cultural opportunities, and recreational activities. Silicon Valley in the area south of San Francisco between Palo Alto and San Jose developed according to this pattern. The area has beautiful mountain scenery, proximity to the Pacific Coast and San Francisco Bay, and a moderate climate; the urban amenities of San Francisco are an hour and a half away; and Stanford University, on the northern end of Silicon Valley, provides a major educational center. Engineering and scientific professionals moved to the area for the quality of life and then founded a host of new companies that drew on Stanford's research resources and the pool of engineering and scientific talent that had been attracted to the area. Despite its lack of natural resources like coal or oil or iron ore, Silicon Valley did have an attractive lifestyle for the human capital that was central to the computer industry.

Analyzing Real Estate in the New Economy

Real estate increasingly will interact with national and international economies and the knowledge economy's accompanying computer and communications revolution. To evaluate the effect of the shift to the knowledge economy on the proposed investment, you will have to ask the following types of questions:

- Is the investment located in an area dominated by major industrial companies or by knowledge-intensive service companies, high-technology manufacturing, and other knowledge service activities such as universities and government?

- Would a massive reduction in communications costs or new communication technology enhance or decrease the attractiveness of the area?

- Would a general change in U.S. trade affect the economy of the area?

- Does the area provide an attractive environment for knowledge workers?

- Does the area have a strong educational system and a well-educated workforce?

Of course, identifying property that will benefit from the development of the knowledge economy and present attractive investment opportunities despite the generally depressed state of real estate always should be done in conjunction with traditional real estate analysis.

Conclusion

The Twenty-first Century: The Century of Human Capital

As the twenty-first century approaches, the knowledge society built on human capital will affect all aspects of life. Old assumptions and rules will no longer apply in a world of computer technology and automation, high-tech products and knowledge services, corporate downsizing and managerial layoffs, working women, an aging population, new consumer attitudes and expectations, Third World competition, and instant communications. The nature of work, social relationships, spending patterns, leisure time and activities, and investment opportunities all will reflect a rapidly evolving new society.

Basic assumptions must be reexamined, new assumptions must be created that are more consistent with current and expected future realities, and ways of thinking and reacting must be made consistent with revised assumptions. Failure to make adjustments will result in inappropriate reactions and decisions in the same way that an American driver's failure to adjust to Great Britain's driving rules leads to unpleasant results.

This book has described this new society and the causes of its development. I hope businesspeople and investors have found that this book has led them to better understand our new society and how to deal more effectively with it in the future.

Appendix A

Human Capital Analysis Methodology

The data for this analysis of human capital relative to total corporate assets came from corporate annual reports, various issues of *Value Line Investment Survey,* Lotus One Source, and ISL stock price books. Because companies are not required to report payroll-related information, most labor cost data were taken from estimates provided by various issues of *Value Line* as a percentage of sales. Both *Value Line* and Lotus One Source provided the number of employees. When labor cost data for a given company were unavailable, a rounded average of the per-employee cost was taken from other companies in the industry, and the total was extrapolated from the number of employees.

The human capital figure—also the hidden equity figure—was calculated by discounting the labor cost figure at 10 percent. That is, the labor cost figure was divided by 10 percent to arrive at the figure applied to the adjusted balance sheet. For example, if a company was estimated to devote 25 percent of its sales revenue to payroll costs, and revenues were $100 million, the total labor cost figure was estimated to be $25 million. The human capital figure was then determined by dividing $25 million by 10 percent to arrive at a figure of $250 million. The bar charts display the average relationship between human capital and the line item termed "related assets"—that is, total assets plus human capital—for each industry. It is hoped that by using at least three companies in each industry anomalies in the data and inaccuracies that can result from using secondary sources have been reduced.

Table A.1   Human Capital Study 1: Companies Included in Human Capital Study

MANUFACTURING

Steel	Forest Products	Petroleum
Bethlehem Steel	Weyerhaeuser	Exxon
USX	James River	Atlantic Richfield
Inland Steel	International Paper	Mobil

Metals	Textiles	Rubber Plastics
Alcoa	Fieldcrest/Canon	Goodyear
Reynolds	Farah	Cooper Tire
Alcan	Belding Hemingway	Goodrich

Chemicals	Automobile	Heavy Equipment
Dow	General Motors	Caterpillar
Monsanto	Ford	John Deere
Millipore	Chrysler	Briggs & Stratton

Household Products	Consumer Durables	Food Processing
Proctor & Gamble	Tonka	Kellogg
Gillette	Jostens	Borden
Clorox	Bassett	Campbell
		Philip Morris

Beverage	Scientific	Electrical
Coca-Cola	Eastman Kodak	General Electric
Pepsico	3M	Motorola
Anheuser Busch	EG&G	General Signal

Publishing	Aerospace	Computer Hardware
McGraw Hill	Boeing	IBM
Time	United Technologies	Apple
New York Times	Lockheed	Hewlett Packard
Washington Post		
Dow Jones		

Pharmaceuticals
Merck
Abbott
Eli Lilly

SERVICES

Utility	Rail	Airline
Consolidated Edison	Norfolk Southern	Delta
FPL Group	Burlington Northern	USAIR
New England Elect.	CSX	Federal Express

Retail Wholesale	Restaurant	Financial Banking
Sears Roebuck	Wendy's	American Express
Wal-Mart	Shoney's	Aetna
K Mart	McDonald's	Great Western
Sysco	Morrison	Morgan Stanley
Tandy		Citicorp
Food Lion		NCNB
Giant		

Hospital Day Care	Hotel Casino Rental	Telecommunications
Kinder Care	Hilton	MCI
Humana	Marriott	AT&T
HCA	Golden Nugget	GTE
	Hertz	

Business Services	Software	Entertainment
Fluor	Computer Science	Disney
Schlumberger	Lotus	MCA
Waste Management	Microsoft	CBS

Table A.2 Human Capital Analysis Study 2: 1989 Balance Sheets of Selected Companies Included in Human Capital Study

	Manufacturing Companies						Service Companies					
	Exxon	General Motors	Motorola	Boeing	Merck	IBM	Consol Edison	Delta	Citicorp	Disney	AT&T	Wal-Mart
Current assets	$16,576	$121,995	$3,915	$8,660	$3,410	$35,875	$1,364	$1,475	$211,155	$2,176	$15,291	$3,631
Property and equipment	60,425	39,126	3,337	3,481	2,293	28,236	8,411	4,478	3,351	3,397	15,919	2,662
Other assets	6,218	12,176	434	1,137	1,054	13,623	575	531	16,137	1,084	6,477	67
Total financial and physical assets	83,219	173,297	7,686	13,278	6,757	77,734	10,350	6,484	230,643	6,657	37,687	6,360
Human capital	51,310	273,380	40,560	60,828	20,963	219,485	8,882	26,969	44,570	18,376	130,410	41,298
Total assets	$134,529	$446,677	$48,246	$74,106	$27,720	$297,219	$19,232	$33,453	$275,213	$25,033	$168,097	$47,658
Short-term liabilities	$21,984	$134,999	$2,751	$6,673	$1,907	$21,700	$935	$1,763	$196,577	$3,036	$12,237	$2,026
Long-term liabilities	30,991	1,665	1,132	474	1,329	17,525	1,322	2,101	23,950	577	12,712	1,327
Total liabilities	$21,984	136,664	3,883	7,147	3,236	39,225	2,257	3,864	220,527	3,613	24,949	3,353
Stated equity	30,991	36,633	3,803	6,131	3,521	38,509	8,093	2,620	10,116	3,044	12,738	3,007
Stated total liabilities and equity	83,219	173,297	7,686	13,278	6,757	77,734	10,350	6,484	230,643	6,657	37,687	6,360
Hidden equity of human capital	51,310	273,380	40,560	60,828	20,963	219,485	8,882	26,969	44,570	18,376	130,410	41,298
Restated liabilities and equity	$134,529	$446,677	$48,246	$74,106	$27,720	$297,219	$19,232	$33,453	$275,213	$25,033	$168,097	$47,658

Note: Balance sheets have been adjusted to include human capital.

Appendix B

The Risk Assessment Guide

This guide can be used to further qualify high-potential, under-valued companies that have been preliminarily identified by the Benjamin Graham quantitative model. Hard-to-quantify factors such as attitudes are important to success in the knowledge economy environment, so the risk assessment guide supplements the Benjamin Graham quantitative model. Using information from such sources as annual reports, public statements, and magazine articles, you can evaluate a company on a scale of 1 to 5 (1=low risk, 5=higher risk) for its future in the knowledge economy. The lower the weighted average from various elements in the risk assessment grid, the higher the company's probability of success in the knowledge economy.

This guide has been developed with the generous and much appreciated assistance of Nick Miller, the president of Clarity, a Boston-based firm that makes information understandable and productive. Clarity provides knowledge design, training, and other human capital development services to pharmaceutical and financial companies and other businesses.

Table B.1   Risk Assessment Guide: Assessing Competitive Strengths and Weaknesses

Characteristic/(Weight)	Highest Risk (5)	(4)	(3)	(2)	Lowest Risk (1)
Customer/market focus	Product-, process-, or engineering-driven.	→			Organize company around serving customer or market.
Quality emphasis	Emphasize quantity of production over quality of production. Products have poor reputation for quality in marketplace.	→			Has established clear framework (customer-based) to define quality expectations. Has developed clear performance standards to address those standards and customer reactions frequently, and responds quickly and decisively to seeing gaps between performance and customer expectations. Strong reputation for quality.
Design of products and services	Emphasis on small number of highly standardized products or services.		→		Primary goal or orientation is to enable customers to customize their own products/services.
Innovation and entrepreneurship	Everything must be approved at headquarters. The "regimental" model. No discretionary funds at work unit level to invest in new ideas. No discretionary time for engineers, etc. to pursue their own projects.		→		Offers opportunities and incentives for innovation and entrepreneurial activity by the individual or at the work unit level. Workers encouraged to work on their own projects (e.g., 3M engineers, 15 percent of time).
Work unit size and direction	Major objective is to grow large to attain economies of scale. Work unit mission is unclear.	→			Has reduced work unit size to fewer than 100 people. Managers' span of direct reports is less than ten. Work unit has a clear mission and measurable goals.

Table B.2 Risk Assessment Guide: Assessing Competitive Strengths and Weaknesses

Characteristic/(Weight)	*Highest Risk* (5)	(4)	(3)	(2)	*Lowest Risk* (1)
Knowledge intensity of processes, work design	Highly labor-intensive, organized like industrial model: high frequency of repetition of same or limited number of highly specified, standard tasks.	→			Highly knowledge-infused. Individual contributors perform varied tasks. Computers or computer-assisted tools perform standard, repetitive tasks.
Use of electronic technology for internal communication	No use of electronic technology for internal communication. Extensive use of paper forms.	→			Aggressive in replacing paper flow with electronic communication (such as Federal Express use of pocket computers for drivers).
Ease of internal information flow	Information and decisions flow through several middle-management layers.	→			Information flow to management or decisions are direct and real time.
Ease of external information flow	Customers must correspond with company on paper regarding all ordering, service, and other issues. Process takes several weeks to complete.	→			Company customers can access information, place orders, etc. directly through company's computers. Use point-of-sale terminals to disseminate product information through telemarketing.
Vulnerability to change (especially change created by information)	Company products and production processes are very knowledge-intensive and company is slow to change.	→			On cutting edge of developing and applying new information and knowledge to key tasks: assessing customer needs, producing products or providing services, and increasing productivity of expensive human resources.

Table B.3 Risk Assessment Guide: Assessing Human Capital Factors

Characteristic/(Weight)	Lowest Risk (1)	(2)	(3)	(4)	Highest Risk (5)
Company reputation	Considered cream of the industry. One of the best two or three firms in the industry to work for.				Clear negative reputation for one or more reasons. Tainted.
Personnel selection	Clear vision of traits and skills required for success at company. Strong recruiting process with careful selection of entry-level employees.				No emphasis on careful employee selection and no vision of traits and skills required for success at company.
Employee education and skill levels	Employee education levels higher than industry norms.				Employee education levels below industry norms.
In-house HR development	Extensive formal and informal in-house programs to upgrade staff skills and awareness on an ongoing basis.				Heavy reliance on apprenticeship methods to train and shape desired performance. Low use of teaching technology to make more efficient.
Turnover/morale/buy-in	Employees identify clearly and thoroughly with management's vision. Turnover low.				Poor employee-management relations. Frequent strikes. High turnover.
Labor relations style	Partnership.				Industrial/confrontational.
Compensation systems	Significant use of gain-sharing, profit-sharing, or employee ownership programs to give employees a stake in productivity and profit. Use of varied and multiple monetary and nonmonetary recognitions that can be awarded quickly, on the spot, by management.				Standard salary administration framework, annual salary reviews, little supervisor discretion in terms of monetary or nonmonetary recognitions and rewards.
Benefits	Offers benefits (such as corporate day care, paternity leave) that appeal to two-income households, etc.				Standard two weeks a year. Nothing special or distinctive.
Personnel systems	Flexible.				Very rigid.

Table B.4 Risk Assessment Guide: Assessing Management

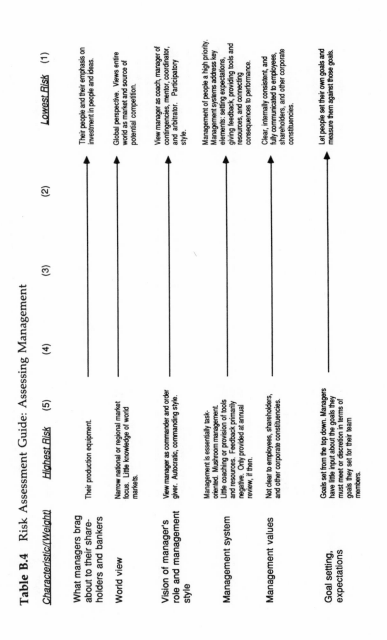

Characteristic/Weight	*Highest Risk* (5)	(4)	(3)	(2)	*Lowest Risk* (1)
What managers brag about to their shareholders and bankers	Their production equipment.	→			Their people and their emphasis on investment in people and ideas.
World view	Narrow national or regional market focus. Little knowledge of world markets.	→			Global perspective. Views entire world as market and source of potential competition.
Vision of manager's role and management style	View manager as commander and order giver. Autocratic, commanding style.	→			View manager as coach, manager of contingencies, mentor, coordinator, and arbitrator. Participatory style.
Management system	Management is essentially task-oriented. Mushroom management. Little coaching or provision of tools and resources. Feedback primarily negative. Only provided at annual review, if then.	→			Management of people a high priority. Management systems address key elements: setting expectations, giving feedback, providing tools and resources, and connecting consequences to performance.
Management values	Not clear to employees, shareholders, and other corporate constituencies.	→			Clear, internally consistent, and fully communicated to employees, shareholders, and other corporate constituencies.
Goal setting, expectations	Goals set from the top down. Managers have little input about the goals they must meet or discretion in terms of goals they set for their team members.	→			Let people set their own goals and measure them against those goals.

Table B.5   Risk Assessment Guide Assessing Management

Characteristic/(Weight)	Highest Risk (5)	(4)	(3)	(2)	Lowest Risk (1)
Attitude about decision making	Emphasis on control, centralized "up through the proper channels" decision making. Bureaucracy. Customer-contact personnel may only take information from a customer or supplier. Must write it up and send to other departments or supervisors for action, taking anywhere from several days to two weeks to resolve.			→	Emphasis on delegation and participation. Adhocracy. Customer contact personnel have information needed and authority to make usual decisions affecting customer (American Express, Federal Express customer service).
Attitude about employees	Personnel are a cost. Primary factors of production are labor, raw materials, and capital. Employees are fungible commodities that can easily be replaced.			→	People are a capital investment. Primary factors of production are people and information. Believe that each employee is a unique individual requiring personal attention.
Attitude about motivation	People must be watched and controlled. Heavy emphasis on quality control by objective third party. Heavy emphasis on reporting of all but the smallest purchases or decisions (such as a can of paint). Heavy emphasis placed on and investment made in the operations manual that prescribes responses for 90 percent or more of potential events. Emphasis on short-term profitability.		→		Values-driven. Employees must be guided by core values. Allow them to make decisions that reflect those core values. Brief manual of procedure. Heavy emphasis on quality control by employee involvement at line level. Emphasis on long-term high-quality performance.
View of personal education	Education is ridiculed as impractical.			→	Managers at all levels place significant personal emphasis on their own education.
Attitude about change	Resists change as long as possible.			→	Reflects desire to be a leader in creating change.
Attitude toward corporated constituencies	Heavy emphasis on one or two constituencies ("the shareholders") to the virtual exclusion of all others.			→	Clearly articulates "who they are" and places great emphasis on balancing their legitimate claims.

Index

Abortion, birthrate reduction and, 67, 68
Acquisitions, in knowledge economy, 51
Additive innovation, destandardization and, 113
Adhocracy, bureaucracy replaced by, 115
Aetna Life and Casualty, 144
Affirmative action programs, 61
Affluence, proliferation of markets due to, 90–91
Aging population, 68–72; savings and, 142, 145–146; services and, 88–90
Agricultural economy, characteristics of, 6, 7, 8; Consciousness I as, 75–76; knowledge acquisition in, 12; labor force allocation in, 15; services in, 16
Agriculture, restructuring and overcapacity of, 48–51
Air travel: for business, 92–93; technology and, 102
Alcoa, 52
AMC, 52
American Express, 139, 144; computer expert system of, 39; global market and, 22; laser-disc players and, 103

Andress, Ursula, 68
Apple, 38, 93
Argentina, debt of, 135
Armed forces. See Military
Artificial intelligence, 38–40
Asahi Life Insurance Company of Japan, 89–90
Asians, in U.S. workforce, 95–96
Atlantic Richfield Co., 109
ATMs. See Automatic teller machines
AT&T, 139, 144; bonds issued by, 149; computers and, 101; picture phones and, 41
Auto industry, global market for, 22
Automated stock selection, 136
Automatic teller machines (ATMs), 105, 122, 136; nationwide networks, 139
Automation, 17, 98, 99; of communications industry, 101–102; of distribution and hospitality sectors, 102–104; in emerging economy, 114–115; of financial services, 104–105, 139; of government, 108–109; of knowledge services, 105–108; of manufacturing, 99–101; of services, 122. See also Computers

185

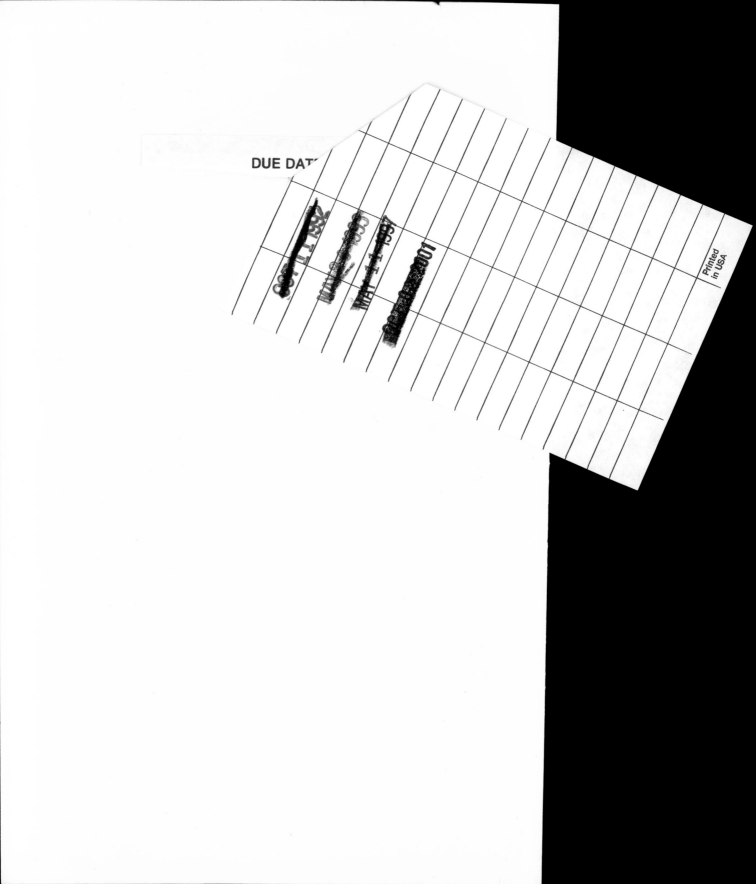

DUE DATE